EXPLORING THE BRECON BEACONS, BLACK MOUNTAINS
AND WATERFALL COUNTRY

A Walker's Guide
Volume I

The Brecon Beacons reach high in heaven in
Pen y Fan and Corn Ddu, the indigo ,
Corniced throne of an intriguing moorland.
Tudor Edwards
The Face of Wales, 1950

OTHER TITLES BY THE SAME AUTHOR:
EXPLORING GWENT (Regional Publications)
MYSTERIOUS WALES (Granada/Paladin paperback;
David & Charles hardback)

★　★　★　★

VOLUME II of EXPLORING THE BRECON BEACONS ... will be
published in due course.

Blaen-y-glyn, Brecon Beacons (C. Barber)

Front cover: *Approaching Sgwd yr Eira (C. Barber)*

Chris Barber

EXPLORING THE BRECON BEACONS
BLACK MOUNTAINS
AND WATERFALL COUNTRY

A Walker's Guide
VOLUME I

REGIONAL PUBLICATIONS
(BRISTOL) LIMITED

First published in Great Britain 1980
under the title 'Exploring the Brecon Beacons National Park'
First revised edition published 1985 under the new title of
'Exploring the Brecon Beacons, Black Mountains and Waterfall Country'

Published by Regional Publications (Bristol) Limited
3 & 5 St Paul's Road, Clifton, Bristol, BS8 1LX
and
5 Springfield Road, Abergavenny, Gwent NP7 5TD

ISBN 0 906570 19 0

Printed by Castle Colour Printers (Berkeley) Limited, Berkeley, Glos.

Contents

The Brecon Beacons, 12

The Waterfall Country, 30

The Black Mountains, 55

Foreword

For a long time there has been a need for this sort of practical guidebook, both to the Beacons and the waterfalls in this area. Chris Barber's book, backed by many years of walking, scrambling and caving in the National Park will add to the enjoyment and appreciation of the discerning visitor who doesn't seek to "do" South Wales in a week, and who will help us care for the countryside.

David Newman,
Capel Twyn, Cantref,
Brecon.

The ridges and peaks of the Black Mountains are not as challenging as some found elsewhere as, for example, those in Snowdonia. They are gentler and softer in their contours and aspect than the sharp crags and often towering profiles of mountains found further north. Therein lies something of the special charm of the Black Mountains.

For most of the year these hills offer safe, relaxed and yet exhilarating ridge-walking—particularly along the north west and north east scarps; but it is as well to remember that even these uplands can be as severe and menacing as any in Britain when blizzards sweep away all the familiar land-marks and snow-drifts lie waist deep. One problem for the hill-walker is that to get to the open uplands he has to make his way through enclosed farmland where public paths are not always obvious.

In this book the author urges his readers to consider the courtesies due to those who live and work in the countryside. The chance of meeting with a farmer on the way to the hills offers an opportunity for a friendly chat to check the correctness of one's route, and perhaps get a useful local weather forecast. Many friendly encounters of this kind are needed to deepen and strengthen mutual understanding between farmers and walkers.

Chris Barber is to be congratulated on writing a guide which will surely be welcomed by all those who already know and love these eastern uplands of the Brecon Beacons National Park, and by all who have not yet been able to explore the Black Mountains and the neighbouring hills and valleys of the National Park.

Wilf Davies,
The Monastery,
Capel-y-ffin.

★   ★   ★   ★

7

Introduction

This guide describes forty-five walking routes in the Brecon Beacons National Park. It covers the Central Beacons group, the beautiful waterfall country and the easterly Black Mountains. An obvious omission is the undulating hill and moorland area to the west of the Beacons known as Fforest Fawr and the Carmarthen Fans. For reasons of perhaps a selfish nature I decided to exclude descriptions of walking routes in this area and leave these more remote and unspoilt hills to the walker who prefers to map read and explore without the aid of a guide book.

The Beacons and Black Mountains are both popular walking areas and the routes described in this guide may help to spread walkers out a bit more, and perhaps serve to reduce erosion problems on some of the traditional routes. These mountains rise to a height of 2,907 feet, and in this area the weather can change very quickly. Common sense dictates the need for waterproof clothing, good footwear, spare food, map and compass. The section on mountain safety has been included to emphasise these precautions.

Place names vary in spelling from map to map and book to book. This guide takes its standard from the Ordnance Survey 1:50,000 map sheets 160 and 161, and the more detailed 1:25,000 Outdoor Leisure Maps covering the central and eastern areas of the Brecon Beacons National Park.

All heights are given in feet, but a comparative metric table is shown at the end of this guide.

I would like to thank everyone who has helped me in the production of this book, especially Tim Pridgeon who helped me compile the original editions of "Walks in the Brecon Beacons" and "Exploring the Waterfall Country" which were published in 1976. My thanks are also due to Roger Millet for preparing the maps. I am also grateful to many other friends who gave me their encouragement, in particular David Newman and Wilf Davies for reading the draft text and making suggestions for its improvement.

Chris Barber,
Llanfoist, Abergavenny, Gwent.
1980 and 1985

★ ★ ★ ★

When visiting this wonderful area
Take nothing but photographs,
Kill nothing but time, and
Leave nothing but your footprints
and goodwill.

Mountain Safety

I must not encumber myself with useless things.
Weight is my enemy, but at the same time I must not forget
anything.

Gaston Rébuffat

The mountains of the Brecon Beacons National Park are grass and heather with little exposed rock, but there are some steep escarpments which should be avoided, particularly in bad weather. Navigation on the ridges is fairly straightforward and an understanding of the topography of the area would prove useful.

Unfortunately some walkers underestimate the dangers of exposure and unsuitable clothing. The following reminders will be generally familiar to most readers, but they are offered as a guide to hill walkers of limited experience.

1. Check weather forecasts and seek local advice.
2. Do not walk alone unless you are confident of your experience and ability.
3. Parties should have good leadership. If forced to split up someone should be left in charge of each group.
4. Plan walks with a generous time allowance. Turn back or head for

Ascending Cwm Sere, below Cribin (C. Barber)

lower ground in bad weather.

5. Take warm and windproof clothes. Even in summer carry a spare sweater.
6. Always carry an Ordnance Survey 1:50,000 or 1:25,000 map and a suitable compass, and know how to use them.
7. Carry reserve food, torch, whistle and first aid kit.
8. In very bad weather seek temporary shelter. To fight the elements is to consume vital energy.
9. In the event of an accident seek the nearest telephone. Dial 999 and state nature of injuries and location. The injured should be kept warm with all spare clothing, and should not be left alone. If possible arrange for one of the party to stay by the 'phone until help arrives.

MOUNTAIN DISTRESS SIGNAL

Six long whistle blasts, torch flashes or shouts are given in quick succession and repeated at minute intervals. To indicate that help is on the way three long signals per minute should be given. This internationally recognised signal should be used only in cases of emergency.

ROUTE PLANNING

Before going to the hills study the map and learn the general lie of the land. Work out 'escape routes' to be used in the event of bad weather. For example it will be noticed that the summits of the Brecon Beacons are fringed to the north, west and east with very steep slopes and fall away more gently to the south. The Roman road shown on the 1:50,000 map (sheet 160) traversing the Beacons from north to south and passing to the east of Cribin is an ideal 'escape route' because it is easily reached from several summits.

TIMING

The times given are the minimum return journey times to suit a party of average ability. It is of course difficult to give precise timings as so many variable factors have to be taken into account, but a fairly accurate estimate is arrived at by allowing one hour for each three miles, and a further hour for each vertical 1,000 feet, but always add a good safety margin.

FOOTPATHS

Not every footpath mentioned is a right of way, but in practice it will be found that most tracks can be walked. Landowners will usually be friendly to walkers who respect the Country Code. The routes in this guide are based mostly on rights of way so few difficulties should be encountered.

MAP REFERENCES

Map references are given thus: (215130) in this guide, but references to place names and natural features are used in most descriptions.

The Brecon Beacons

The valley of Usk lay misted and golden under the rising sun and the air was as crisp as frosted wine. Away to the west the pasturelands rolled to the Brecon Beacons, their peaks mist shrouded and purple with threats.

Alexander Cordell

This is an impressive group of hills dominated by the flat tops of Pen y Fan and Corn Dû with the sharp ridge of Bryn Teg leading to the summit of Cribin.

Hills or mountains? Snowdon is only 654 feet higher than Pen y Fan and, although the Beacons are relatively easy of access, they still demand the respect that must be accorded to other areas of high peaks and great precipices. However inviting the day may be, the walker should not approach the Beacons carelessly. Commonsense dictates the wearing of adequate footwear and clothes, and the provision of food, map and compass.

ACCESS RESTRICTIONS

In the Brecon Beacons access through Cwmgwdi to Cefn Cwm-llwch is restricted when the army firing range is in use. Information on firing times can be obtained from the Mountain Centre, Libanus, or at the National Park Information Centre, Glamorgan Street, Brecon. The range is easily avoided by following the diverted footpath to the east. The path starts at a small car park immediately north of the range.

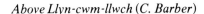

Above Llyn-cwm-llwch (C. Barber)

11

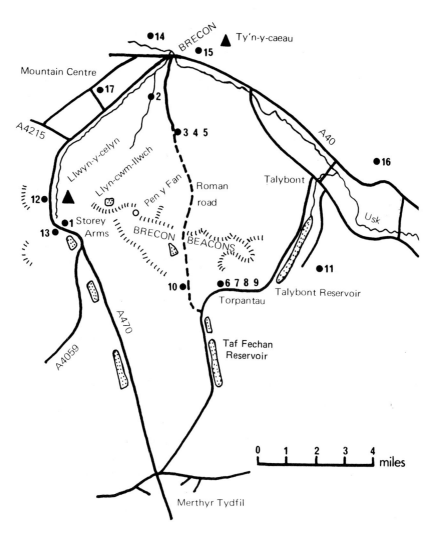

●14 BRECON ▲ Ty'n-y-caeau
●15

Mountain Centre

●17 ●2

A4215

●3 4 5

Llwyn-y-celyn

Llyn-cwm-llwch

Pen y Fan

Roman
road

Talybont

A40

●16

●12 ▲

●1 Storey
13● Arms

BRECON

BEACONS

Usk

●11

10 ● ●6 7 8 9

Torpantau

Talybont Reservoir

A470

Taf Fechan
Reservoir

A4059

0   1   2   3   4
└──┴──┴──┴──┘ miles

Merthyr Tydfil

START OF ROUTES 1 TO 17—BRECON BEACONS

12

The Ascent of Pen y Fan

The thrill of a mountain first seen
or of a first climb attempted, remains
for each newcomer a unique sensation.

Geoffrey Winthrop Young

Route 1
From Storey Arms (2½ hours)

Pen y Fan is the highest point in the Brecon Beacons (2,907ft.). It can be reached from Storey Arms, on the A470 Brecon — Merthyr road, in about an hour, but this direct 'tourist' route is probably the least interesting of the many ways to the top. Storey Arms, once a youth hostel, is now a youth adventure centre. At one time part of the building was a transport café, and the disappearance of this place of shelter and refreshment is regretted by Beacons walkers. There is plenty of parking space about half-a-mile down the road towards Methyr where toilets are available.

Walk half a mile south-east from Storey Arms (towards Merthyr) to reach an obvious track leading off left to a stream and waterfall. The track crosses the stream and leads upwards to an obelisk bearing the sign of the National Trust. Thirty minutes' steady walking up the path, which has been eroded to a barren highway, brings you to Bwlch Duwynt, the saddle between Duwynt to the right and Corn Dû (2,863ft.) to the left. From here there is a choice of two routes: either a rocky scramble over the top of Corn Dû or an easier walk through the saddle and around the right flank of Corn Dû, where the tracks rejoin.

From this point the track steepens to the summit plateau of Pen y Fan, which is marked by a trig' point obelisk.

Care must be taken on this summit, as on all the northern Beacons summits, because of the near-vertical 600ft. north face. The view ranges from the Black Mountains to the Prescelly Hills of Pembrokeshire (now Dyfed) and from Exmoor to Plynlimon. Westwards stands Bannau Brycheiniog, highest point of the Carmarthen Fans, beyond Fan Fawr. Llyn Syfaddan (Llangorse Lake) is to the north-east and Cader Idris, highest mountain between Pen y Fan and Snowdon, may reveal itself far to the north-west in very clear weather.

The return journey can be made by retracing steps directly to Storey Arms or making a circuit via the summit and ridge of Corn Dû, above the little lake of Llyn-cwm-llwch. From the top of Corn Dû, descend the steep north-west ridge with care until easier ground directly above the lake is gained. From this point, swing in an arc to the top of Y Gyrn and down the grassy slopes to the road by Storey Arms. The return via Y Gyrn is not recommended to inexperienced walkers and should not in any case be undertaken without map and compass.

Route 2
Via Cwm-llŵch (3 hours)

To reach Cwm-llwch from Brecon, take the road opposite the Drovers' Arms on the A40 near the western outskirts of the town. Travel past Ffrwdgrech Lodge and over the bridge of Pont Rhyd Goch. Below this bridge the river Llwch cascades through the woods to join the Afon Tarell lower down. The cascades are known as the Ffrwdgrech Falls and are well worth a visit. After a mile the road becomes a rough track which ends in a clearing (where you can leave your car) between the two spurs of Pen Milan and Cefn Cwm-llwch.

From here, follow the rough track past Cwm-llwch Farm, now restored and used as a school weekend mountain base (mountain rescue equipment and telephone). Over a stile, and the track continues upwards past a National Trust sign, climbing steeply over a hump and then more gradually towards the high circular hollow below the flat-topped summit of Corn Dû. For the unsuspecting walker the surprise comes at the last minute. Immediately below the looming hulk of Corn Dû the scene is suddenly peaceful and inviting; here is the pool of Llyn-cwm-llwch, a small lake of glacial origin. At one time it was called the lake of Cwm-llwch dingle and also Pwll-y-doctor (the doctor's pool) after a famous scholar, Dr David John Rhys, who lived for many years in the old farmhouse further down the valley.

The Tommy Jones obelisk below Corn Dû (C. Barber)

According to local tradition the pool is supposed to be bottomless. Students from Hereford College of Education recently investigated the depth and found it to be about fifty feet in the centre. It was once said that if the bell ropes from Llanfaes Church, Brecon, were tied together they would not reach the bottom.

Another legend describes how some men and boys dug a gully through the northern edge of the pool in order to let the water out. A man in a red coat, sitting in an armchair, suddenly appeared on the surface and threatened (in Welsh) 'If I get no quiet in my place, I shall drown the town of Brecon.' Thus it was recorded that any attempt to tamper with the pool will result in the flooding of Brecon.

The twelfth-century chronicler Giraldus described Llyn-cwm-llwch as a mysterious spring which rises in the Beacons: 'Deep, but of a square shape like a well and although no streams enter it, trout are sometimes found in it.' It is in fact a corrie lake, left behind when glacial ice receded from the north facing cwms of the Beacons.

The track climbs steeply from the pool through zig-zags to the ridge of Corn Dû and the Tommy Jones obelisk, a memorial to a small boy who ventured too far from Cwm-llwch Farm where he was staying with his grandfather.

The inscription reads:

This obelisk
marks the spot
where the body of
Tommy Jones
aged 5 was found.
He lost his way
between Cwmllwch
farm and the Login
on the night of
August 4th 1900.
After an anxious search
of 29 days his remains
were discovered Sept. 2nd.
Erected by voluntary
subscriptions.

W. Powell Price
Mayor of Brecon 1900.

The obelisk provides a useful landmark in misty weather, for on reaching the stone the walker knows exactly his position on the ridge from the summit of Corn Dû to Pen Milan.

From the obelisk the ridge ascends gradually and then quite steeply for the last 100 yards. In a strong wind it is advisable to keep clear of the slopes dropping steeply into the cwm, for a sudden gust may blow you off balance. The last part of the slope is best taken by striking diagonally upwards to the right to follow a line of crude steps worn by countless feet, to arrive suddenly on the flat top of Corn Dû.

The adventurous walker may discover a narrow track some twenty feet below the summit leading across the north face of Corn Dû at the foot of the upper band of rock. In order to miss out the summit of Corn Dû and make directly for Pen y Fan itself this route serves as a useful and impressive short cut, but there are many who freeze at the prospect of such a traverse.

To complete the Cwm-llwch circuit, walk to the northern edge of Pen y Fan summit and descend the steep track (with care in muddy conditions) down the ridge of Cefn Cwm-llwch. In icy or very wet weather it is sometimes advisable to join the ridge by returning to the col between Pen y Fan and Corn Dû and pick up a track leading diagonally down to Cefn Cwm-llwch. In winter conditions an ice axe is often essential for a safe descent of the initial steep slope.

The path down the centre of the ridge leads to Cwm Gwdi, where an army firing range used to be located, but this is no longer in use and access is now unrestricted. To return to the Cwm-llwch car park it is necessary to leave the crest of the ridge after a mile and descend gradually over open ground to Cwm-llwch stream and farm.

Routes 3, 4 and 5:
Pen y Fan via Cwm Cynwyn

To reach Cwm Cynwyn travel south-east from Brecon via Cantref to the start of the Roman road just beyond Bailea Farm (040240). Soon after the tarmac road surface ends the track arrives at a gate which gives access to the rising ground of Bryn-teg. From this point there are three alternative routes to Pen y Fan; ascent can be made by one and descent by another.

Route 3
Via the Roman road (3 hours)

Walk (or cycle—this route has always been a favourite with cross-country cyclists) along the Roman road for about three miles until the 'gap', the highest point, is reached. Having gained the top of the pass, with a view of the Neuadd Reservoirs to the south, follow the track north-west up the flank of Cribin to the summit or, for an easier walk, diagonally to the saddle between Cribin and Pen y Fan. The final slope is steep enough to demand the use of an ice axe in winter conditions.

North-east face of Pen y Fan (C. Barber)

Route 4
Via Bryn-teg (3 hours)

Take the track which leads up the ridge of Bryn-teg and heads straight for the summit of Cribin. The going is fairly easy until the famous 'snout' is reached, rising steeply for the final 300ft. to the top. This sharp arête is an obvious feature of the Beacons when viewed from a distance at certain angles and has led some writers to describe Cribin as 'the Welsh Matter-horn', a nickname it shares with Cnicht in Snowdonia. The steepness of the ridge is not too severe if it is tackled steadily, and the view from the crest is a just reward.

To avoid Cribin and its snout, find a narrow track which crosses the north face and leads directly to the saddle between Cribin and Pen y Fan. It is a very exposed traverse and the poor condition of the track where it crosses the scree gullies calls for a cool head and steady footwork, but it is one of the most enjoyable routes in the Beacons and affords fine views of the towering north-east face of Pen y Fan. Perhaps the track was engineered by shepherds as a short cut; the name 'goat track' seems to be used by a lot of people. The author was once startled by a fox which raced past him on one of the sharp bends. By using this route it takes a mere ten minutes to reach the usual route to Pen y Fan, as opposed to thirty minutes over the top of Cribin, making it an excellent short cut; surely its original purpose.

Route 5
Via Cwm Sere (3 hours)

This is a little-known route from the gate at the foot of Cwm Cynwyn to the foot of Pen y Fan's north face. Head south-west from the gate to follow a track beside a long stone wall. The track gradually climbs the eastern side of the valley along the lower slopes of Bryn-teg; it is narrow and diverse in places but eventually reaches flatter ground near the top of the valley and not far from the source of the Sere stream (Nant Sere).

Above is the col (saddle) between Cribin and Pen y Fan. In the centre of the col will be seen the line of a diagonal track leading down into the cwm. To reach the start of this track it is necessary to walk over the rough stony ground at the bottom of the gullies below Pen y Fan. When the diagonal track is reached it provides a surprisingly easy way up to the col where the ordinary route to the top may be joined.

Routes 6, 7 and 8
Pen y Fan from the south-east

The southern approaches to the Beacons are less impressive than those from the north, but it is interesting to climb mountains from all directions. Routes 6, 7, 8 and 9 start from a parking area (055175) half a mile beyond the remains of Torpantau station on the east side of the road, in the southern part of the Beacons not far from the northern end of the Taf Fechan Reservoir. In the days when trains ran to this remote spot the walker could complete many routes without having to rely on his car, and the lighted station and the train chugging up the track were welcome sights to the walker descending from the rainswept summits. The station buildings became unsafe and were demolished several years ago.

To reach the starting point, take the Pontsticill road from Merthyr Tydfil or Cefn-coed-y-cymmer on the A465 Heads of the Valleys road. Turn right immediately after the Taf Fechan Reservoir, pass the site of the station (050168) and carry on for half a mile to the parking area.

Route 6
Via the Roman road (3 hours)

Traverse the hillside west of the parking area, meet the Roman road and follow it to the crest of the pass. Climb the track to the north-west which contours the southern flank of Cribin, or climb Cribin itself, and make your way westwards along the obvious route to Pen y Fan. Return by the same route.

Route 7
Via Garn Fawr (3 hours)

Strike north-west from the parking area over Garn Fawr to reach the north facing escarpment of Craig Cwm-oergwm and then the crest of the pass on the Roman road. From here, proceed to Pen y Fan as in Route 3 or Route 6. Return by the same route.

Craig y Fan-ddu from the north (W. T. Barber)

19

Route 8
Via Craig y Fan-ddu (3 hours)

From the parking area, follow a well-defined track up the steep slope northwards to the ridge of Craig y Fan-ddu which, halfway along its length, turns north-north-east and becomes Craig Fan-las. Walk along the ridge until the halfway point approximately has been passed, then head north-west again across peat-covered Gwaen Cerrig-llwydion, popularly known as the 'moon country', to the ridge of Craig Cwmoergwm. From here, a well-worn track leads to the 'gap' (the crest of the pass on the Roman road) and Pen y Fan. The walker has the option of climbing or bypassing Cribin.

Popular Circuit Routes
Route 9
The Blaen-y-glyn circuit (3 hours)

This is an enjoyable half-day walk with good views and several items of interest: waterfalls, cliffs, the remains of a wartime bomber and the peat hollows of the 'moon country'. The starting point is as for Routes 6, 7 and 8: the crest of the rise on the road half a mile or so beyond Torpantau station towards Talybont.

A well defined track leads from here towards Craig y Fan-ddu. The track crosses the Nant Bwrefwi at the top of an impressive 40ft. waterfall. From here, walking past the remains of a stone wall, look to the east to see the Sugar Loaf and Skii rid Fawr rising into view. In the south another conical hill thrusts up from the skyline: this is only a pile of black slag.

The path rises steeply but is well-stepped near the top. Abruptly, to the left, the twin table-tops of Corn Dû and Pen y Fan rise into view, and the long escarpment of Craig Gwàun-taf. Follow the path, keeping the valley on your left until you reach a cluster of rocks on your right (useful for shelter). Now strike north-east to meet the escarpment of Craig Fan-las where a good path follows the edge. Ahead in the distance are the peat hollows of the 'moon country'. Now cross the rocky gully of the Caerfanell, which in spate makes a fine waterfall into the valley below. The path is hard to follow over the next section, but contour around the head of the valley keeping fairly high and soon the path improves.

At last the edge of the north escarpment is reached. From here there are fine views towards Radnorshire, and to the west is the north-east face of Pen y Fan with the snout of Cribin rising in front of it. The track crosses the 'moon country'. Keep to the lower track, dipping in and out of the peat hollows. This acid peat that covers large areas of the plateau and gently sloping southern slopes is composed of decayed plants that grew here thousands of years ago.

On reaching the edge of Cwâr y Gigfran cliffs look down the first gully and you will see the scattered remains of a Wellington bomber on the rocks below. In the gully bed is one of the engines and the other will be found on the plateau above the cliffs. It is possible to find chromium parts that still show no sign of rust.

At the end of Cwâr y Gigfran (raven's quarry) there is an interesting view-point. A depression behind a large block (the 'balcony') gives fine views over the shoulder of the Allt-lwyd ridge towards the Black Mountains and the Sugar Loaf. Below are the steep slopes of Gwalciau'r Cwm with Nant Cynafon running through the forestry plantation. Now descend the ridge towards Blaen-y-glyn. A narrow track leads around underneath the 'balcony' to another good vantage point and sheltered resting place.

Follow a definite groove (possibly an old quarry track) first steeply and then gently. On reaching a fence the track descends into the valley. Near the stream there is a stone with a bold inscription: G. H. 1845. Keep to the left bank of the Caerfanell until the path crosses the stream by a large block in mid-water. The river descends in a series of tumbling waterfalls with the largest cascading into a small amphitheatre, now a favourite spot for picnickers. Blaen-y-glyn Farmhouse, which was demolished some years ago, once stood above the remains of the stone bridge. There is a Forestry Commission walk laid out in this beauty spot.

Route 10
Circuit of the Beacons (5 hours)

Take the Pontsticill road from Merthyr Tydfil or Cefn-coed-y-cymmer, on the Heads of the Valleys road (A465), and drive straight past the big Taf Fechan Reservoir to the Neuadd Reservoirs over two miles further on. There is a small car park at the end of the road near the gate to the reservoir buildings (032179) and another at the Forestry Commission picnic site (037170).

From the reservoir buildings car park, follow a track leading down to the valley towards a stile. Descend to cross the stream (sometimes difficult in wet weather). Follow the line of telegraph poles and then take the track to the edge of the forestry plantation. The slope above is quite gentle but on reaching the end of the plantation there is a steep but short ascent to the ridge.

Once on top of the ridge make for the trig' point of Twyn Mwyalchod, a good viewpoint. From here the track leads northwards, following the edge of the ridge, with fine views of the Neuadd Reservoirs. To the south are the hills of the industrial valleys and to the east the isolated hills of Skirrid Fawr and Sugar Loaf.

The beautiful valley of Cwm Crew is later passed on the left. Notice the moraine, or glacial debris, near its top end.

Now the ridge becomes narrow and flat, rather like a causeway, as it passes over Rhiw yr Ysgyfarnog and Craig Gwaun-taf to reach Duwynt (not named on the 1:50,000 map but marked 824 metres).

This hill has no definite summit but it is a good viewpoint, providing a fine view of Bannau Brycheiniog to the far west and the wild moorland of

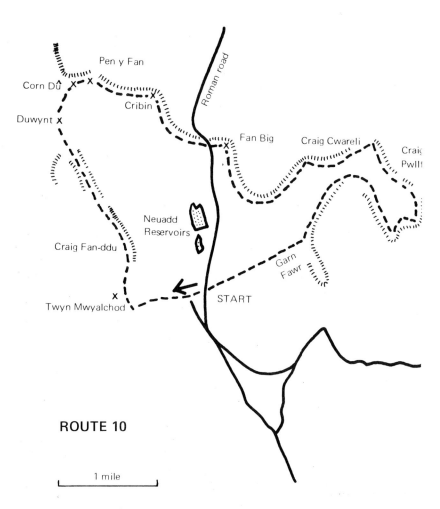

ROUTE 10

1 mile

CIRCUIT TRAVERSE OF THE BRECON BEACONS

Fforest Fawr.

A short descent leads to the saddle, where a track heads down to Storey Arms. From the saddle either continue over Corn Dû summit or take the short cut traverse which leads directly to Pen y Fan.

Walk to the southern end of Pen y Fan summit, that is, directly towards the Neuadd Reservoirs far below, and begin the tricky descent. It is badly eroded and great care is needed.

Descend to the saddle between Pen y Fan and Cribin; the steepest climb on the entire route is now ahead. When stopping to rest, turn to view Pen y Fan's mighty north-east face. Cribin's summit is just beyond the top of the slope. From the top, look down the 'snout' on the northern end and then, turning south, walk down the slope to the 'gap' where the Roman road reaches its highest point. From here, the Roman road can be followed back to the starting point if desired, thus offering a semi-circuit option and a usefully rapid descent in case of deteriorating weather.

From the 'gap', climb eastwards to the summit of Fan Big (not marked on the 1:50,000 map); the slope is steep but not as long as the approach to Cribin. A pony path goes off to the right, bypassing the summit and providing a more gradual approach to the ridge. The summit of Fan Big is a fine viewpoint and is marked by a small cairn. Notice the 'diving board', a popular spot for a photograph.

Head south-east again over Craig Cwm-oergwm. The 'moon country' of Gwaen Cerrig-llwydion can be seen on the other side of the big valley, eastwards. An old quarry is soon reached; its rocky depressions provide shelter for a meal break, but please respect the area, particularly the wet-weather emergency shelter in the centre of the quarry. Take your litter away.

Continue along the path around the horseshoe-shaped valley. Behind, the three main peaks of the Beacons stand proudly; ahead, the track follows the edge of the ridge, and being more rocky than many in the Beacons suffers less erosion. As the corner is turned, Llangorse Lake and the Black Mountains come into view. Follow the ridge, now in a north-easterly direction, to the end of the next curve, where the track starts to descend. Leave the main track here and cut off to the right, heading for a cairn on the skyline about a mile away (763 metres on the 1:50,000 map). From the cairn, make for the trig' point obelisk (762 metres on the map). This is the plateau of Craig Pwllfa, a viewpoint with a wide panorama.

Leaving the trig' point, continue to the east (facing towards the distant Sugar Loaf) passing on the side of the track part of an old aircraft engine. Soon you reach a large cairn. This is known locally as 'the old man' and it marks the end of the summit plateau. The cairn has grown considerably over the years. Directly below is the old farmhouse of Nant-llanerch which was once a popular youth hostel. In the distance is Talybont Reservoir with the hill of Tor y Foel standing behind it.

Head south along the blunt end of Craig y Fan, following the track on the edge with a view of a narrow valley below (Cwm Tarthwyni). At the end of this ridge, turn to the west. The return journey now begins.

Below is the afforested valley of Cwm Cynafon. Swing around a tight corner to reach the end of Cwâr y Gigfran. At the end of this ridge is the 'balcony', a large block of stone which provides a sheltered resting place.

Continue north-westwards along the ridge. The path is well defined, but take care because there are steep cliffs below. On reaching the final section of cliff, look down to see the remains of a Wellington aircraft, which failed to clear the hill during World War II.

Now cut back across the edge of the 'moon country' to reach the head of the valley. From there, head upwards to gain the edge of Craig Fan-las and a good track.

On reaching a rocky gully carrying a stream, strike south-west away from the ridge. Follow a vague track across open country to reach two cairns at Garn Fawr, one square and tidy and the other one a tumbling heap. There are interesting rock formations at this point which provide useful shelter from the wind.

Continue south-west to reach a pile of rocks. This is probably the largest area of scattered rocks in the Beacons. From the lower end of the rocks follow a path leading towards the forestry plantation on the other side of the valley.

The path leads down to a stream and soon the reservoir buildings are in sight. On this walk, you have maintained height until the last moment; a gradual descent into the valley brings you to the Roman road; follow it down to a gate. Take a path to the left, cross a stile and a gravel track and descend to the starting point.

Outlying Peaks

Route 11
Tor y Foel (1 hour short route, 3 hours long route)

This peak stands to the east of the Beacons and south of Talybont, a village in the Usk valley on the road south of the river between Brecon and Crickhowell, the B4558. It is best climbed from the mountain road which leaves the B4558 about half a mile east of Talybont at 117225 and climbs steeply around the western slopes of the hill. There are fine views of the Beacons and Talybont Reservoir from this road.

Where the road flattens out, a suitable parking place will be found on the left; it is from here that the short ascent may be made to the 1,806ft. summit. The return journey can retrace the approach or, to lengthen the walk, can be made by descending the east-facing ridge to meet a track

Tor y Foel from the east (W. T. Barber)—the Brecon and Abergavenny Canal in the foreground

which leads after a little over a quarter of a mile to a road. Turn left along the road for 200 yards and take a footpath on the left which passes below a forestry plantation and past a canal bridge. The track contours around the lower northern slopes of Tor y Foel and climbs gently to the starting point.

Route 12
Craig Cerrig-gleisiad (1½ hours)

The summit of this rocky escarpment is easily reached from the picnic site just south of Llwyn-y-celyn Youth Hostel on the A470 Brecon-Merthyr road. The well-worn path leaves the picnic site, which is on the west side of the road, climbs the steep ridge and follows a broken stone wall. The view is extensive. Return by the same route or continue along the ridge to the more gradual slopes which descend to the cwm, where a track follows the stream back to the road.

The cliffs are protected as a nature reserve for arctic-alpine flora. Scrambling on the cliffs is not allowed and in any event would be dangerous because of their friable, vegetated nature.

Route 13
Fan Fawr (1½ hours)

The track to Fan Fawr starts directly opposite the adventure centre at Storey Arms on the A470 Brecon-Merthyr road. The summit of Fan Fawr, at 2,409ft., is the highest point of the mountainous tableland known as Fforest Fawr, an area which has four tops over 2,000ft. (Bannau Sir Gaer and Bannau Brycheiniog, both higher than Fan Fawr, are in the adjoining region of Mynydd Dû, the Black Mountain in the west—not to be confused with the Black Mountains north of Crickhowell). Return over the outward route.

Viewpoints

Route 14
Pen-y-crug (2 hours)

This walk starts in Brecon. From the cathedral, follow Upper Chapel Road, turning left just past the 30 mph speed limit derestriction signs to follow the course of a Roman road for half a mile. Beyond a barn on the right, turn left up a lane and continue to a gate. From this point, an obvious path leads over open ground to the top of Pen-y-crug. The height of the trig' point is 1,088ft.

The well preserved earthworks on the hill are the remains of an Iron Age hill fort. The Roman fort of Y Gaer is visible two miles to the west. The view is very wide, ranging from the Black Mountains in the east over the Brecon Beacons to the Carmarthen Fans (Fforest Fawr and Mynydd Dû) in the west.

Return is by the same route.

Route 15
Slwch Tump (1 hour)

This walk starts in Brecon, immediately above the Brecon County Hospital in the north of the town. A lane branches east off Cerrigcochion Road and leads to Slwch Tump (Slwch Camp on sheet 160), which is a fine viewpoint for the town and surrounding country. Return is by the outward route.

The Beacons from Pen-y-crug (W. T. Barber)

The legend attached to Slwch Tump is that Elyned, youngest of twenty-four daughters of Brychan, an ancient prince of Brycheiniog, suffered martyrdom there. A chapel named after Elyned once stood on the north side of the hill. An old name for the hill was Penginger, a corruption of Pen Cefn-y-gaer (the summit of the ridge of the fortification).

Route 16 (sheet 161)
Allt yr Esgair (1½ hours)

This long, narrow hill is situated two miles north-west of Bwlch, a village on the A40 eight miles east of Brecon. It is easily reached by turning north-wards off the A40 on the crown of the sharp bend half a mile west of the village. A track, marked 'Roman Road' on sheet 161, starts on the left at 140223 where the road makes a sharp turn to the right. Follow the track up the middle of the ridge to the summit, which provides good views of the Brecon Beacons and Llangorse Lake (Llyn Syfaddan).

Return by the outward route.

Route 17
Mynydd Illtyd and the Mountain Centre

A visit to the Brecon Beacons is not complete without a stop at the National Park Mountain Centre, which is open every day of the year except Christmas Day. The approach roads are well signed from the A40, A470 and A4215.

This fine building is situated at 1,100ft. on the moorland hills of Mynydd Illtyd. The purpose of the centre is to provide a focal point where visitors can obtain information and refreshment before moving on to other parts of the National Park. Facilities include an information office, shop, lounge, picnic room for those who carry their own food, refreshment room and toilets, also picnic tables outside. The broad panorama of the mountains, seen through the large windows, makes the lounge a fine place to relax. The Mountain Centre was opened on 1 June 1966 by the Secretary of State for Wales, the Right Hon. Cledwyn Hughes, MP.

Nearby is the church of the famous Celt St. Illtyd; his grave, marked 'Bedd Illtyd' on the Ordnance Survey maps, is reputed to be here. Legend has it that Illtyd owned an unusual animal, half horse and half stag, which carried his provisions from market.

A mile or so along the road to the west, opposite a small pool, is the ancient mound of Maescar Castle. The foundations of the round tower are probably thirteenth century, and the castle may have been built to guard the old road to Ystradfellte, where there is a similar overgrown mound known as Castell Côch (Red Castle).

Approaching Cribin (C. Barber)

The Waterfall Country

Strangers who come afar, having heard of the fame of this valley, may see but little in it, from expecting too much and in too little time; most of the beauties lie out of the direct route, and require some search.

William Weston Young

This will always be my favourite corner of the National Park, and I have visited the many waterfalls and caves numerous times during the past twenty years—taking photographs and sketching in all climatic conditions. Standing behind the shining liquid curtain of Sgwd yr Eira on a moonlit night one summer, I decided to write about the area around Ystradfellte for the benefit of visitors seeking the beauty and mysteries of the Hepste, Mellte, Nêdd, Pyrddin and Sychryd. These five rivers drain the uplands of Fforest Fawr and combine close to the village of Pont Nedd Fechan.

This is a fascinating area with impressive waterfalls, moss covered boulders, wooded slopes, curious rock formations, intriguing cave systems and towering cliffs.

Some of the paths are high and often slippery, so stout footwear is essential. Children must be kept under control for a slip on certain sections could be fatal.

The falls are at their best during or after wet weather, so waterproof clothing is desirable, particularly when walking behind Sgwd yr Eira on the Hepste river when there is a lot of water coming over the falls.

A visit to the falls during a period of hard frost or heavy snow makes an interesting expedition— even calling for the use of axes or crampons. The falls when frozen are very beautiful, Sgwd yr Eira being very impressive. Sgwd Gwladys and Sgwd Einion Gam on the Pyrddin river are the most likely to freeze because they face east. The other falls mostly face south or west.

Lower Clyn-gwyn Falls, Afon Mellte

30

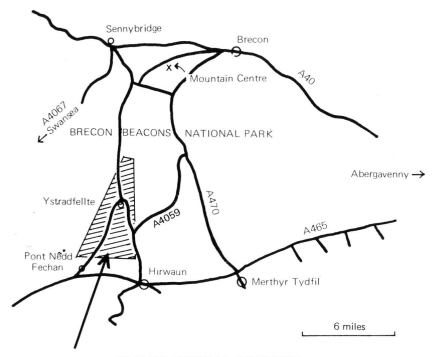

THE WATERFALL COUNTRY

Approaches to the area

From Brecon   Take the A40 westwards to the roundabout. Follow the A470 up through the Tarell valley for about nine miles, turning right on the A4059 immediately after the first reservoir. The road traverses beautiful moorland country. Ystradfellte is signposted to the right after about six miles.

From the Brecon Beacons Mountain Centre   Take the road westwards from Mynydd Illtyd Common, on which the Centre stands, towards Heol Senni. A turning just before the village is signposted to Ystradfellte, and the road follows an interesting route through the Senni Valley and up the 'Zig-Zags', as this mountain pass is generally called. A large standing stone, Maen Llia, is passed on the left just over the summit; the road descends gradually to Ystradfellte.

From the Heads of the Valleys road (A465)   Leave the A465 at the Glynneath junction and take the B4242 to Pont Nêdd Fechan. Turn left at the Dinas Hotel for Ystradfellte.

The Mellte Valley

Ystradfellte

Situated in the Mellte Valley at an altitude of 825ft., this tiny hamlet is at the very heart of the waterfall country. At the centre of the village on the crossroads is the New Inn, where cavers and walkers will be found discussing routes to waterfalls and limestone caverns on most weekends. Camping is allowed in the field opposite the inn. Nearby is the village post office and shop.

The church has little of antique interest, being largely restored in 1870, but the gnarled yew trees that surround it are believed to be 800 years old. The largest is eighteen feet in circumference and is higher than the church.

North-east of Ystradfellte, at the confluence of the Afon Llia and the Afon Dringarth which form the Afon Mellte, are the remains of Castell Côch (Red Castle). This was a small castle built of Old Red Sandstone boulders taken from the river bed.

One mile south of the village is a small youth hostel, providing accommodation for members of the Youth Hostels Association and offering an ideal base for cavers and walkers exploring this area.

Many visitors have difficulty in pronouncing the name Ystradfellte: try USTRADVETHTUR, which though only an approximation is better than some alternatives that the author has heard.

During its journey to join the river Neath or Nêdd near Pont Nêdd Fechan, the Mellte sometimes passes underground through channels in the limestone, leaving the pebbles on the bed above to give the appearance of an unfinished road. When you enter the village from the east, where the road crosses the Mellte, you may see the dry river bed, but after periods of heavy rain the subterranean channels are unable to carry the entire flow and the bed then becomes covered with water.

The first impressive feature on the Mellte is the cave system of Porth yr Ogof where the river disappears underground for nearly three quarters of a mile.

Route 18
Porth yr Ogof (15 minutes for quick visit)

Drive for about half a mile south from Ystradfellte and take the first turning on the left (just before reaching the youth hostel). A narrow lane winds steeply down to the floor of the valley. On the left is a car park with toilet facilities. Cross a stile at the far end of the car park and follow a well-worn path (often slippery in damp weather) down to a shallow gorge where the river goes underground into the wide mouth of Porth yr Ogof.

Many of the early visitors to this area considered Porth yr Ogof to be the

Porth yr Ogof, main entrance (C. Barber)

outstanding feature of the district and described it with great enthusiasm but often poor accuracy. Earlier names have included Porth Mawr (Great Gateway) and Cwm-porth Cavern. At one time it was also called White Horse Cave. This name stems from the calcite streaks on the wall about 150 feet inside the main entrance that resemble the head of a horse.

An immediate impression is made by the size of the entrance, certainly the largest in Wales. Experienced cavers are able to enter the underground system at fifteen different points, but only two entrances are easily accessible to the casual visitor. These are the Main Entrance and the 'Tradesman's Entrance' which provides a view of the Mellte on its way into the main system.

The entrance chamber can be explored without a light, but only as far as the White Horse Pool. A passage on the right of the entrance chamber gives access to the main passage of the river. The ceiling of this passage is quite remarkable for it is completely flat for an area of about 6,000 square feet and is supported only at the edges. There are very few formations in the cave, but the experienced caver will wish to explore Hywel's Grotto which is reached by crawling on the stomach along sandy passages and through pools of water. Unfortunately some of the formations there have been destroyed by thoughtless people.

After a period of heavy rain, when the Mellte is in flood, the main entrance becomes impassable, but it is impressive to watch the water hurtling into the cave. During exceptional conditions the water has been known to reach the roof. Large trees have been swept into the cave and at one time the body of a horse was carried into the main chamber.

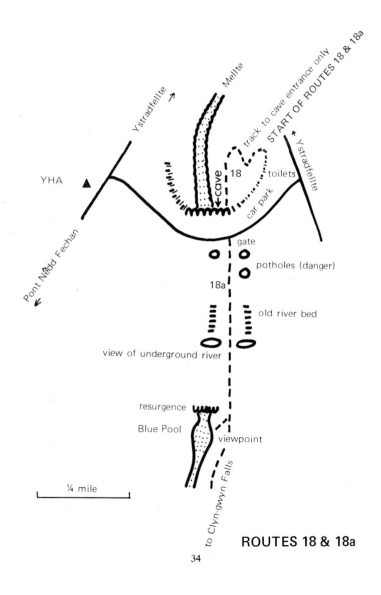

ROUTES 18 & 18a

Through the years several people have been drowned in Porth yr Ogof, some of them experienced cavers. It is emphasised that a journey through the system is a serious undertaking and that any exploration beyond the entrance chamber should be carried out only by properly equipped and knowledgeable parties.

Route 18a
The resurgence of the Mellte (20 minutes)

After inspecting the entrance of Porth yr Ogof, return to the car park and cross the road to pass through a gate on the other side to follow the long abandoned river bed of the Mellte. Soon you pass three pothole entrances to the cave. Take care when peering down, for a caving ladder is necessary to descend the forty-foot drop. Continue along the footpath for another 100 yards to pass between two collapsed entrances which provide glimpses of the river Mellte on its journey underground. Over the top of the next rise you come to the resurgence, where a large rock platform provides a splendid view of the dramatic water exit and the pool below. The total length of the underground river from the main entrance to the resurgence is about 300 yards and the drop in level approximately twenty feet.

Route 19
The Clyn-gwyn Falls (3 hours)

From the car park near Porth yr Ogof, follow the east bank of the river Mellte via the resurgence (as previously described). After a mile a foot-bridge is reached. Here there is a choice of route. By crossing the bridge it is possible to visit the first two falls and reach the best viewpoint for the second fall, but in order to reach the lower fall from here, and if you wish to visit Sgwd yr Eira on the Hepste river, it is necessary to stay on the east bank of the Mellte.

In order to avoid a river crossing and to visit all four waterfalls, carry on past the footbridge to follow a waymarked path. Soon you are looking down on Sgwd Clyn-gwyn, generally referred to as the Upper Fall.

The waymarked path avoids the most difficult and dangerous ground and inexperienced walkers should follow this recommended route for several serious and fatal accidents have occured in this valley in recent years.

Follow the waymarks to reach a view of the middle fall which is known as Sgwd Isaf Clyn-gwyn. The curved top of the fall resembles a miniature Niagra and it is particularly impressive after heavy rainfall.

William Weston Young, a nineteenth-century writer, described the scene:
"Now right, now left its devious course descends,
In grandeur wild, the broken waters flow
Then in a large unbroken mass extends
And swiftly pass the polish'd rocks below."

Continue along the path to reach a finger post where a track leads down to the third fall, Sgwd y Pannwr, which although smaller than the other two is still quite picturesque. The pool below the fall is reputed to have once been the home of a huge fish that refused to be caught.

From here you can retrace your steps to the starting point at Porth yr Ogof car park or from the finger post (previously mentioned) continue to Sgwd yr Eira. (This fall can also be reached from Penderyn. See Route 21).

Route 19a
Sgwd yr Eira from Sgwd y Pannwr
(1½ hours extra)

From Sgwd y Pannwr follow the waymarked path to the junction at the finger post. This high ground provides a fine view, embracing the whole of the Mellte Valley northwards to Fforest Fawr and southwards to the Vale of Neath.

From the wooded ridge between the Mellte and the Hepste rivers a path descends a series of steps (take care for they are slippery when wet) to the foot of Sgwd yr Eira where it is possible to follow the path behind the fall and stand with a great curtain of thrashing water cascading over your head. (For a detailed description of the fall see page 42).

Further down the river are the Lower Cilhepste Falls which descend in a series of steps and form very long rapids.

Return via the steps to the high ground above Sgwd yr Eira and either retrace your steps to the car park at Porth yr Ogof or cross a stile to follow a path through a conifer plantation to reach Gwaen Hepste car park where a track leads down to join a path above the Mellte, about quarter-of-a-mile from Porth yr Ogof car park.

Sgwd Isaf Clyn-gwyn (W. T. Barber)

Sgwd y Pannwr (C. Barber)

Route 20
The Clyn-gwyn Falls: alternative approach (20 minutes)

This is an easy, direct approach.

From Ystradfellte, drive approximately one and a half miles south on the road to Pont Nêdd Fechan. After passing a filling station and shop you soon reach a wide parking space on the right hand side of the road (919106). A rough track leads from here to the ruins of Clyn-gwyn Farm. A well-trodden route bearing right leads to Sgwd Isaf Clyn-gwyn, and the left hand track heads for the river bank and Sgwd Clyn-gwyn.

By following the latter track a short distance northwards and crossing the footbridge, Sgwd y Pannwr and Sgwd yr Eira may be reached (pick up and follow Routes 19 and 19a).

WARNING — There have been bad accidents in recent years on these paths. Do not be complacent. Tread carefully and watch young children.

The Hepste Valley

Penderyn

The Hepste Valley is best reached from the small village of Penderyn, one and a half miles north of Hirwaun. It is the centre of an important quarrying industry and in the nineteenth century there was also an iron foundry here.

River Hepste

Three streams rise on the sandstone mass of Fforest Fawr: Afon-y-waen, Nant y Cwrier and the Nant Llwch. They unite to form the river Hepste, which is often confused with the Mellte.

Apart from the impressive waterfall of Sgwd yr Eira, the Hepste is remarkable for the way that it disappears underground for quite long stretches. People often assume that the river has 'dried up'. From the bridge (945112) on the road linking Ystradfellte with the A4059, the river bed is usually dry, the river having disappeared underground nearly two miles upstream. Only in times of flood, when the subterranean stream is unable to cope with the rush of water, will the Hepste flow along this dry bed. Beneath the sandstone pebbles in the river bed is the limestone through which the water has worn underground channels.

ROUTES 19, 19a, & 20

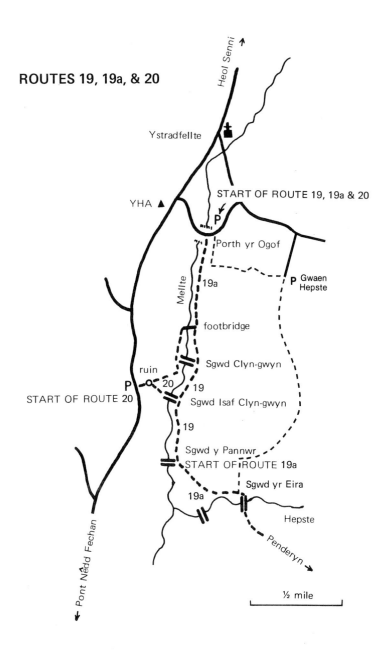

39

Routes 21 and 21a combined start
Sgwd yr Eira from Penderyn (3 hours)

Sgwd yr Eira is perhaps the most famous of all the waterfalls in these valleys, due to the fact that it is possible to walk behind the broad curtain of water. However, despite its fame, many people try in vain to find a route to the fall and it has thus gained a reputation of being hard to reach.

At Penderyn leave the A4059 where a side road makes an elbow with the main road (near a seat and just beyond a garage). Fifty yards up this road, at the end of a row of houses, is a public footpath signpost pointing the way through a gate. Ignore the track on the left which leads to Tor Foel Farm. Continue through another gate. On reaching a junction follow the track leading downhill. After two more gates, the route descends gradually into the valley of the Hepste.

Pass on the left the rusting remains of a corrugated iron shed; soon a wire fence with concrete posts is reached. From here there are two routes, Routes 21 and 21a continuations.

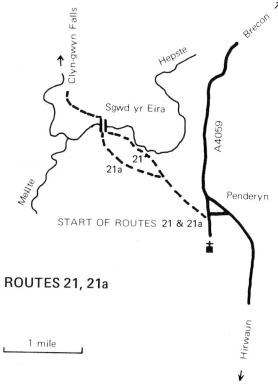

40

Sgwd yr Eira (W. T. Barber)

Route 21 continuation
Through the Hepste Valley (difficult)

Descend past the fence into the valley and follow a narrow track on the left bank of the Hepste. Care is needed in many places for a false step could send you tumbling into the river. This is no route for the timid walker. The valley now becomes very narrow with steep sides and the path is hard to follow in places. Sometimes it is necessary to scramble over fallen trees, with the river rushing by one hundred feet below. At last, the track descends to the river; turn another corner and the fall is directly below.

Route 21a continuation
Across the moors (often boggy)

From the wire fence, head towards the trees on the left and follow a well-worn track heading west. This route will keep you out of the steep and difficult Hepste Valley until the final descent to the fall. Follow the track across the moorland for about half a mile, eventually reaching a large conglomerate boulder. This is a useful landmark, for Sgwd yr Eira is directly below this point and can be plainly heard.

Sgwd yr Eira (The spout of snow)

As you descend the steep slope of the valley side to the level of the river, the first sight of this fall is quite breathtaking. In very wet weather the fall may appear as a broad sheet of foam, but generally there are three separate falls. Of course the greatest prize of all is to see the water completely frozen.

The top of the fall is overhanging and the water is thrown clear of a rocky ledge about three feet wide, which is a pathway behind the curtain of thrashing water and spray. This is the only path from one side of the valley to the other and years ago farmers drove their sheep along this route.

It is a fine experience to pass behind the fall and stand on the edge looking through the water, but take care for the wet rock can be very slippery.

The valley of the Hepste below Sgwd yr Eira is known as the Devil's Glen and is the setting of tales about ghosts, fairies, goblins and witches.

To return to Penderyn, retrace your steps or follow the alternative route back to the head of the valley. Otherwise, take the route from Sgwd yr Eira over the ridge to the Mellte Valley and the Clyn-gwyn falls instead of returning directly to Penderyn (Route 19).

The Pyrddin and Nêdd Valleys

Waterfalls . . . .
To see them in perfection the traveller must wait for rain, a
delay that will be amply repaid by the gratification which the
scenery must produce. For this he need not wait long as the
country is seldom two days without showers.

Richard Warner

Pont Nêdd Fechan and the Nêdd

This small village is situated in the valley of the river Neath or Nêdd three
miles south-west of Penderyn and one and a half miles north-east of
Glynneath. The river above the village is commonly known as the Nêdd
Fechan, or Little Neath, but as many visitors will be using the Ordnance
Survey 1:50,000 sheet, which does not specify 'Nêdd Fechan', references
throughout this book will be to the Nêdd and will thus be consistent with the
map.

Local industries have been silica mining, limestone quarrying and coal
mining, and until recently there was a silica mine operating in the nearby
Sychryd valley. In the more distant past a gunpowder works (closed
December 1931) was situated on the bank of the Mellte, and a few years ago
a cannon that was used to test the gunpowder was removed to Brecon
Museum.

It is claimed that Welsh hats were once made in the village.

Routes 22 and 22a combined start
Falls of the Pyrddin and Nêdd (3 hours total for both)

The track to the falls starts from the old bridge behind the Angel Hotel at
Pont Nêdd Fechan. Follow the river upstream past impressive overhangs.
Before long the valley becomes much flatter and wider. Notice on the right
some large holes, indications of mine workings. Just beyond are the remains
of a bridge and some buildings.

The track now hugs the side of the river and is much narrower. A junction
is reached. The more obvious track rises steeply through the woods, and if
you follow this route you will climb high above the river and face a slippery
descent down the side of a wooded gully to regain the river bank. The
narrow track to the right follows the river bank all the way.

The confluence of the Nêdd and Pyrddin is soon reached by either route.
Here there is a sturdy metal bridge over the Pyrddin. Cross it and take
Route 22 continuation to the falls of the Pyrddin or Route 22a continuation
to the falls of the Nêdd.

Route 22 continuation
Pyrddin: Sgwd Gwladys and Sgwd Einion Gam

Having crossed the bridge, follow the track to the left. Climbing gently through the woods you are soon looking down on the first fall, a minor one which is apparently unnamed. The track falls to a platform which provides a convenient viewpoint.

Further along the track the next fall, Sgwd Gwladys, will soon be heard. It is not possible to see the fall from the track until the top of a rise is reached; suddenly, you are level with the top of the fall. Keep well clear of the edge, for this is a dangerous situation. It is possible to descend from the platform overlooking the fall to river level where a good view is obtained near a fallen tree.

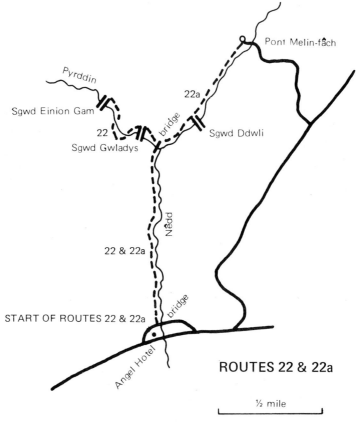

ROUTES 22 & 22a

½ mile

Sgwd Einion Gam (C. Barber)

45

Sgwd Gwladys is sometimes known as the Lady's Fall and the name is reputedly derived from Gwladys, one of the twenty-six daughters of Brychan, King of Brycheiniog in the fifth century.

The fall is similar in appearance to Sgwd yr Eira, with a jutting ledge and a space behind the water where it is sometimes possible to stand. There is no track leading on to the opposite bank.

Just beyond the fall is a large boulder which was once a rocking stone. Its weight has been calculated at seventeen tons and it was once so delicately poised that a push of the finger would move it. Early tourists claimed to crack nuts, gathered in the neighbouring woods, beneath it. During the building of the railway in the Neath Valley, a gang of workmen vandalised the remarkable stone by overturning it.

Further upstream and very difficult to approach is the waterfall of Sgwd Einion Gam. A cliff on the north side of the Pyrddin makes it necessary to ford the river somewhere near Sgwd Gwladys and again later to avoid the steep sides of the valley. This should not be attempted when the river is high. The route upriver to this hidden fall does not follow a distinct path and it is rare to see anyone else making the journey.

Soon you reach a high, narrow gorge and further progress is prevented by a wall of rock and the fall of Sgwd Einion Gam. The water rushes over a rocky ledge and changes its direction to plunge sheer into the pool below. From here the eddying waters hurry over the rocks into a second and larger basin. The total height of the fall is about seventy feet and it is impressively situated in a deep ravine.

Gam may be translated as crooked and the fall is sometimes known as the Crooked Fall, but Einion's identity is uncertain.

Route 22a continuation
Falls of the Nêdd

From the metal bridge at the junction of the Pyrddin and Nêdd follow the track along the bank of the Nêdd to the right of the bridge. Passing through an avenue of trees, the track is broad and easy to follow. After a few hundred yards a point is reached where the river appears to flow through a gateway of rock rather like a sluice gate. Just beyond, the track leads to a wooden bridge crossing a narrow ravine. This is Pont Nant Llechau, which some years ago was lifted into place by an RAF helicopter as part of a foot-path improvement organised by the National Park Warden Service.

Five minutes upstream is the fall known as Sgwd Ddwli, which is im-pressive when the river is flowing fast. Two other minor falls a short way upstream are usually referred to as the Upper Sgwd Ddwli falls. Beyond the last fall the path continues until it reaches a small car park and picnic area (Pont Melin-fâch). This is the starting point for Route 23.

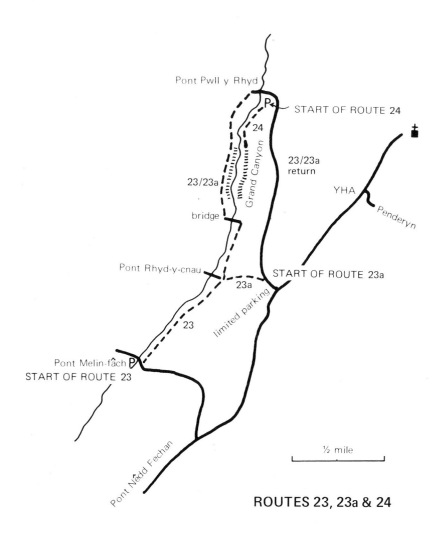

Pont Pwll y Rhyd

START OF ROUTE 24

24

23/23a
return

Grand Canyon

23/23a

YHA

Penderyn

bridge

Pont Rhyd-y-cnau

START OF ROUTE 23a

23a

limited parking

23

Pont Melin-fâch
START OF ROUTE 23

½ mile

Pont Nêdd Fechan

ROUTES 23, 23a & 24

Routes 23 and 23a
The Grand Canyon walk

The main route, Route 23, involves a journey along the course of the Nêdd from Pont Melin-fâch to Pont Pwll y Rhyd. The path, a right of way, is not easy to follow and calls for scrambling over boulders and the negotiation of steep slopes and rocks. It is a strenuous route for which boots are necessary. Route 23 is joined by Route 23a at Pont Rhyd-y-cnau and the two continue as one.

Route 23
Pont Melin-fâch to Pont Rhyd-y-cnau
(3½ hours for complete journey)

To reach the starting point, an attractive picnic site and car park (918106), turn off the Ystradfellte - Pont Nêdd Fechan road just under a mile south of the parking spot for Route 20. The car park was built by volunteer working parties, and the young people involved received a Prince of Wales Award for their efforts.

From the car park, cross the bridge and follow the right bank northwards. The track is not well used and there may be obstacles. Soon the valley becomes very picturesque, and the track passes below an overhanging rock to climb gently to the upper bank from which the narrowing gorge can be seen. At a stile, the lower path should be taken. It is not easy to follow, but the general rule is to strike upwards when the going becomes difficult; you will find a track on the upper bank. Eventually a little bridge, Pont Rhyd-y-cnau, is reached. This is where Routes 23 and 23a combine.

Route 23a
Alternative approach to Pont Rhyd-y-cnau
(3 hours for complete journey)

Take the first turning right after leaving Ystradfellte (travelling south); after a quarter of a mile approximately, stop by a grass track on the left. There is parking space for two or three vehicles. The track winds steeply down into the valley and provides a fine, direct approach to Pont Rhyd-y-cnau, where Routes 23 and 23a combine.

Routes 23 and 23a combined
Pont Rhyd-y-cnau to Pont Pwll y Rhyd

From the bridge, follow the right hand (eastern) bank upstream. A well-trodden track meanders along the riverside and through the trees. After a stream-crossing and a stile, the valley narrows then opens into a small amphitheatre: Pwll Dû, the black pool. This is the resurgence of an underground river; from beneath an overhanging mass of rock the water flows towards the main stream. The path continues along the bank, soon climbing again and then dropping gradually to a tricky final descent over boulders to the riverside. The river bed, dry except after a period of heavy rain, is reached along a grassy path. If the water is flowing, strike upwards to follow the top track; otherwise, it is interesting to walk along the river bed and savour the eerie atmosphere, noticeable particularly to the lone walker.

The adventurous walker may choose to continue through the gorge along the river bed, but others will make for the upper track on the right which soon descends to the river again and leads to the bridge where the river reappears. Notice below the bridge the curious holes worn out of the rock.

The route crosses the bridge to the other bank and heads upwards towards a ruined farmhouse. From this building, take the lower track through the field from which the gorge is soon seen again. The track reaches the gorge, now deep and narrow. Some enthusiasts travel the complete length of the gorge at river bed level. It is possible to descend into the gorge at a point where the river disappears again—the clue to the location is the absence of the sound of water—but it is more easily entered from the top end (see Route 24).

The path drops to a gravel track and a gate, beyond which the valley opens out and the gorge ends. A bridge is crossed—Pont Pwll y Rhyd—and a small parking area reached. There is easy access to the gorge from here.

Routes 23 and 23a
Return to starting point

From Pont Pwll y Rhyd, it is usual to return to Pont Melin-fâch or Pont Rhyd-y-cnau by road. After the difficulties of the outward journey, the hard surface and open aspect make a pleasant contrast. A mile or so from Pont Pwll y Rhyd, notice on the left a large and deep swallet hole, caused by the collapse of the roof of an underground chamber.

Route 24
Top entry to gorge (Grand Canyon)

From Pont Pwll y Rhyd parking place, follow the track on the left bank of the river, passing immediately on the left a hollow containing the entrance to Bridge Cave. Continue through a hole in the fence, passing a small cave entrance on the left and reaching the river bed. Walk along the bed for twenty yards. Just beyond a large square boulder, take the track on the left bank and climb through the trees to the left of a small cliff face.

At the top of the bluff, turn immediately right and descend to a platform from which the chasm can be viewed. In very wet weather water flows along the normally dry river bed, cascades into this deep fissure and enters a cave system, emerging 150 yards downstream at White Lady Cave. The underground passage was first explored in 1960.

Make your way down on the left of the chasm. The track leads past an overhanging cliff on the right below which a scramble descent can be made into a cave. There is a deep pool inside. The Grand Canyon, the popular name for the gorge, is now entered, and a damp descent leads to an awkward eight-foot drop which overhangs slightly. Below, the river reappears through the tunnel-like entrance of White Lady Cave. Further to the left, the small entrance to Town Drain Cave can be seen.

Progress beyond this point is wet and difficult, and return to Pont Pwll y Rhyd by the outward route is advised.

The Sychryd Gorge

To reach the Sychryd (dry ford) Gorge, which is about a mile east of Pont Nêdd Fechan, drive past the Dinas Hotel in the village and cross the narrow bridge over the Mellte. Look for the parking area on the left below the impressive rock outcrop known as Craig y Ddinas. This huge wedge of mountain limestone is about 150 feet high and stands between the Mellte and Sychryd rivers at their confluence; old guide books often refer to it as the 'fortress precipice'. Its isolation makes it an object of interest to the geologist and rock climber, and the slabs to the right of the main buttress are used by local outdoor activity centres for climbing instruction. Eighteenth-century engravings show the degree of change wrought by quarrying at Craig y Ddinas.

A steep path on the right leads to the top of the rock and from the broad plateau there is a good view towards Glynneath.

Route 25
Sychryd Gorge and Falls (1 hour)

Follow the track past the parking area and around the back of Craig y Ddinas into the Sychryd Valley, passing towering ivy-hung walls of limestone on the left. Soon a clearing is reached. On the right, across the river, is a curious mass of rock known as Bwa Maen, the bow of stone. Underneath the curving overhang is the slit-like entrance of a cave, with another smaller entrance on the right. This is Y Ffwrn (the oven), one of many places throughout Britain associated with the legend of the sleeping King Arthur and his knights, always ready to spring into action to save the country from disaster.

At the end of the track there used to be a ramp leading up to the old Silica mines beyond. Unfortunately it became unsafe and was demolished a few years ago. However the adventurous walker will make an easy scramble up the rocks beside the tumbling water providing the river is not in flood. On the left is Will's Hole. Beware! there is a 50-foot pothole inside.

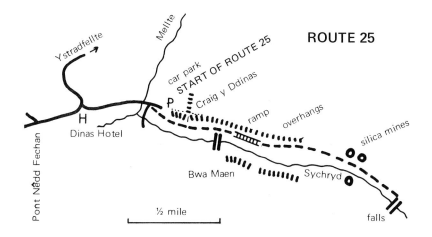

The valley above is wild and impressive. An overhanging roof, extending for nearly twenty feet, provides an excellent place to shelter on a rainy day. Soon you will pass the entrance to another cave on the left. Ogof Coed y Ffyrnau, which consists of a series of small passages leading in the direction of Will's Hole.

Below the site of the old mine workings are a couple of small waterfalls. It is inadvisable to explore these workings for they are considered unsafe.

The track rises through the trees. Soon you are looking down on another fall which is easily reached by descending the grass bank. This fall is the final point of interest in the valley. Retrace your steps to return to the car park below Craig y Ddinas.

Route 26
The Waterfall Roundabout (5 hours)

A strong walker may wish to visit all the waterfalls in one day, a tiring expedition which should not be attempted by those unused to walking in rough country.

Starting at the Angel at Pont Nêdd Fechan, walk east for about a mile to Craig y Ddinas and follow the track to the left of the crag in a north-easterly direction. A gradual ascent leads across the moorland slopes of Moel Penderyn to the wooded valley of the Hepste. Descend to Sgwd yr Eira and pass behind the fall to follow the track to the Lower Cilhepste Fall. Now continue through the woods to reach the Mellte Valley and visit in succession Sgwd y Pannwr and the two Clyn-gwyn falls. Cross the footbridge just beyond the Upper Clyn-gwyn Fall to follow the right bank of the Mellte and then a track via the ruins of Clyn-gwyn Farm to the Ystradfellte—Pont Nêdd Fechan road.

Take the road south for about half a mile to reach the lane leading to the picnic site at Pont Melin-fâch. Follow the right bank of the river to the falls of Sgwd Ddwli and carry on to the confluence of the Nêdd and the Pyrddin. From the metal bridge follow the right bank of the Pyrddin to visit Sgwd Gwladys and Sgwd Einion Gam. Retrace your steps to the bridge and cross it to follow the right bank of the Nêdd back to your starting point at Pont Nêdd Fechan.

ROUTE 26

THE WATERFALL ROUNDABOUT

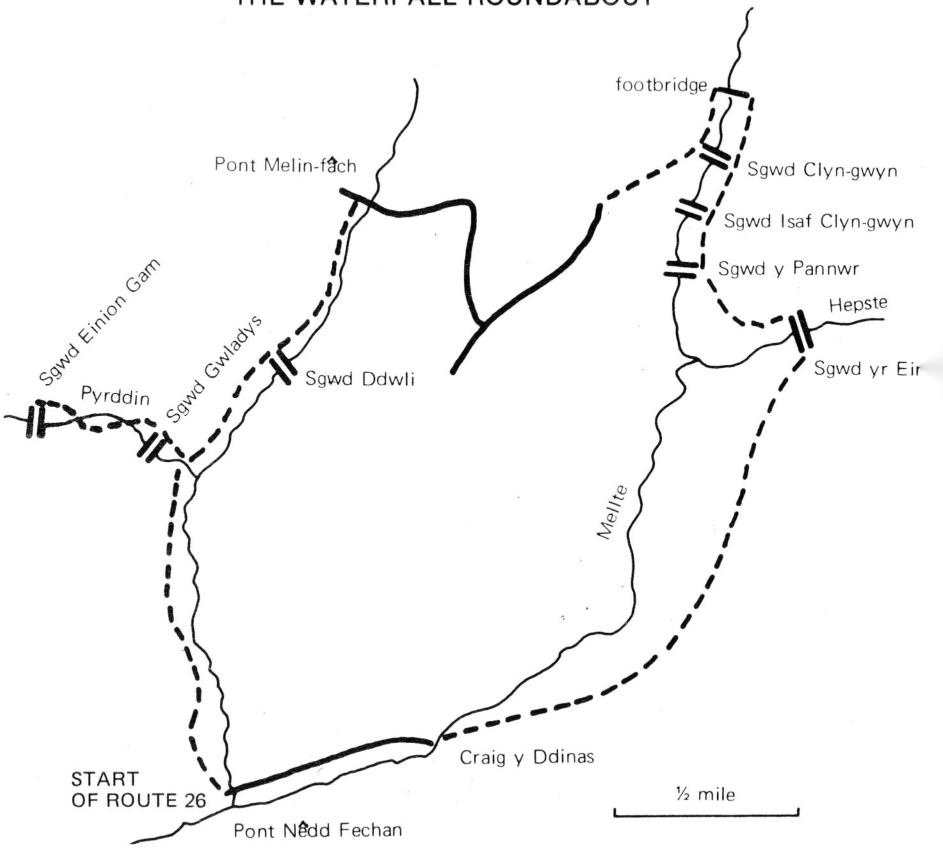

footbridge

Pont Melin-fâch

Sgwd Clyn-gwyn

Sgwd Isaf Clyn-gwyn

Sgwd y Pannwr

Hepste

Sgwd Einion Gam

Sgwd Gwladys

Sgwd Ddwli

Sgwd yr Eir

Pyrddin

Mellte

Craig y Ddinas

START
OF ROUTE 26

½ mile

Pont Nêdd Fechan

Sgwd Isaf Clyn-gwyn (C. Barber)

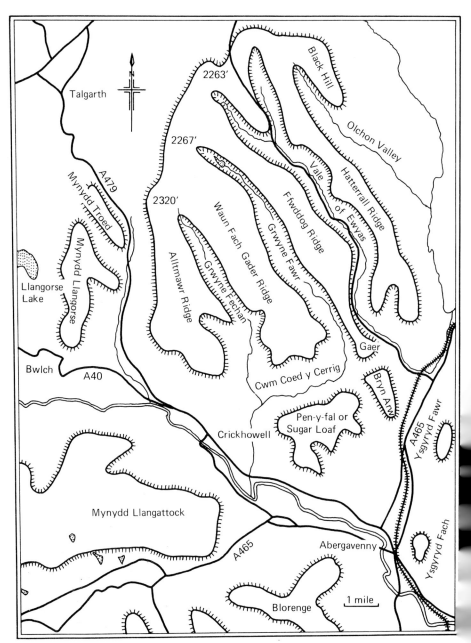

THE BLACK MOUNTAINS AND OUTLYING HILLS

The Black Mountains

The Black Mountains of the Welsh - English Border are a singularly unspoilt group of long and lofty ridges separated by valleys of diversified charm, descending steeply towards the Wye on the northen side, and on the southern side less abruptly towards the Usk.

P. Thoresby Jones

Travelling towards the County of Gwent one may pick out on the skyline a long black ridge. For many visitors this is their first sight of these mountains, and the reason for their descriptive name is self-evident. Some say it was the Saxons who provided the name for they always saw the mountains from the eastern side of the Wye. Very few Saxons crossed the river into Gwent and lived to return.

It was A. G. Bradley who described the ridges and valleys of the Black Mountains as "eighty square miles of complete, uncompromising solitude". This may well have been so at one time, but now the "Blacks" are much more popular with walkers and pony trekkers, so that summer days are rare when one can roam without meeting other walkers or catch sight of a line of riders moving across the skyline.

A plan view of the Black Mountains resembles a right hand placed flat on a table with the fingers spread apart. This is an easy way to remember the layout of the five ridges and four valleys of this compact group of hills.

Waun Fach—2,660 ft.

The highest peak of the Black Mountains can be reached by several good routes and those described here are three of the best. As a viewpoint Waun Fach is not very spectacular; the view from nearby Pen y Gader is better.

Route 27
From Pengenffordd (3½ hours)

This route starts at the highest point of the Crickhowell to Talgarth road (A479). There is limited parking by a telephone box, but the Castle Inn, ½ mile south, has a good car park (ask for permission). From Pengenffordd follow a lane to the right of the telephone box. This leads up through the trees to a tarmac road. Turn left at the end of the road to take a public footpath which is signposted to indicate your way up a deeply rutted track to the start of the ridge Y Grib.

At the start of the ridge—on the right—are the remains of Castell Dinas, which was built as a fortification in the late 12th century. Follow a direct line up the centre of the ridge. After the initial steep gradient the ridge becomes gradual until it ascends in a series of humps with the mass of Waun Fach looming above. To the right one looks down into the lovely Rhiangoll Valley and across the long line of the Pen Allt-mawr ridge.

After the second hump a short descent leads to a shoulder where various tracks meet to provide alternative routes to this point from the valleys on either side. From here the track is clearly defined and follows the left hand side of the ridge. Alternatively one may ascend the crest of the ridge, but the lower track provides a more direct route to the next dip in the ridge.

On the next hump the track passes over boulders. Now follow the ridge for better views and a more exhilarating position. Soon a small cairn is

Northern Escarpment of the Black Mountains (W. T. Barber)

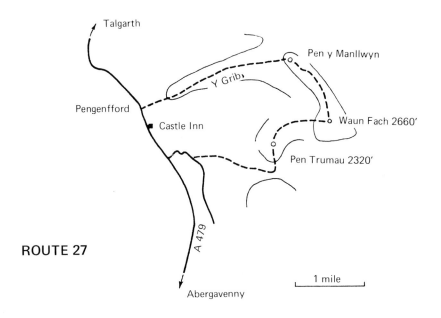

ROUTE 27

Talgarth

Pen y Manllwyn

Y Grib

Pengenfford

Castle Inn

Waun Fach 2660'

Pen Trumau 2320'

A 479

1 mile

Abergavenny

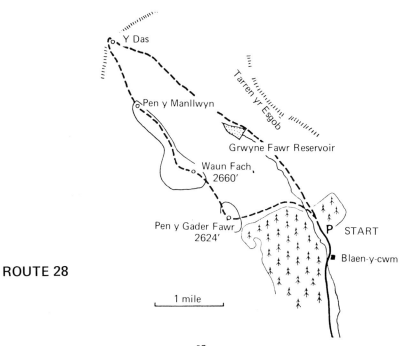

ROUTE 28

Y Das

Pen y Manllwyn

Tarren yr Esgob

Grwyne Fawr Reservoir

Waun Fach 2660'

Pen y Gader Fawr 2624'

START

P

Blaen-y-cwm

1 mile

reached and the ridge becomes flatter and broader. Just before reaching the head of the valley on the left it is necessary to leave the main track which skirts around the head of this valley to follow a less trodden path up the slopes of Pen y Manllwyn. When you reach the path following the centre of the ridge, turn right towards Waun Fach.

Away to the north one can appreciate the solitude of the terminal plateau of the Black Mountains. On the skyline to the east is the Hatterrall ridge which forms part of Offa's Dyke long distance footpath.

Soon you reach the summit of Pen y Manllwyn marked by an upright stone. The track is inclined to be boggy, but is well defined. After passing a cairn the summit of Waun Fach is reached (2 hours average time). The base of the old trig' point and a cairn marks the summit. The meaning of Waun Fach is "little bog" and it often lives up to its name.

From the west side of the plateau a path descends to the ridge of Pen Trumau; on reaching the blunt end of this ridge go down to the col and from a large cairn follow the track to the right. This offers an easy descent to a tree lined sunken lane and then a tarmac road. Turn right and soon after a left hand track takes you past the Cwm Fforest Riding Centre. At a sharp bend turn right to cross a stream, and after about half a mile a left turn leads to the Castle Inn and the main road.

Route 28
From Blaen-y-cwm (3 hours)

Drive up the Grwyne Fawr Valley to reach the Forestry Commission picnic site north of Blaen-y-cwm at 251286.

Walk up the road to a gate. Pass through and where a stream flows in a gully on the left—at the end of the forestry plantation—cross the river Grwyne (sometimes difficult if in flood). Follow the track on the right of the stream which zig-zags up the slope to lead across open country away from the stream and towards Pen y Gader Fawr. After a while the track is hard to follow, but the ascent is fairly gradual.

Below is the lonely Grwyne Fawr Reservoir with its high dam bridging the narrow valley. On reaching the upper plateau the hump of Pen y Gader Fawr is seen directly ahead. The summit is marked with a cairn, and this is possibly the best viewpoint in the Black Mountains (2,624ft.).

Now follow a well worn track to Waun Fach across the peaty ridge, jumping across a wide gully close to the summit plateau of Waun Fach. Again the summit is marked by a cairn and the base of the old trig' point. Continue along the path to Pen y Manllwyn and then the north escarpment. From here are fine views of the upper Wye Valley, the Begwyns and Radnor Forest. Turn right here to follow the track back to the Grwyne Fawr Reservoir; from there a broad track, originally built during the construction of the dam, descends to the starting point.

Grwyne Fawr Reservoir (C. Barber)

Walks in the Llanthony Valley

Route 29
Cwmyoy Church and The Darren (2 hours)

It should be noted that rocky sections of the route are not suitable for young children or poorly shod walkers.

Cwmyoy Church is situated on the eastern side of the lower part of the Llanthony Valley and is well worth a visit. The ancient building clings precariously to the hillside, and the tower leans at a crazy angle with the nave walls bulging outwards to lean in the opposite direction. It would appear that these structural defects resulted from subsidence several centuries ago. Parking for cars at this location is very limited.

At the south end of the church a path leads to a metal gate through which the track is followed. Turn immediately right up a path signposted "Graig". On reaching another gate keep left to pass a wooden building. At the next gate keep straight on heading towards the base of the Darren cliffs. After passing through a metal gate, by a stream, keep to the left hand side of the valley to reach a "standing stone" about 4ft. 6in. high (1½ metres), which is either an erratic, perhaps, or marks an ancient way.

At a point where the valley floor is covered with boulders, cross to the right hand side of the valley. Follow a vague track, threading your way between boulders and hawthorn trees, up through this "Valley of Rocks".

The track improves and soon the towering Darren cliffs are reached. Now go left of a stone wall to follow the crest of a ridge on the left side of the valley and then descend into the bottom of the valley towards the end of the cliffs. Continue beside a stone wall and just beyond the end of the valley a track leads upwards to give a zig-zag ascent of the hillside above. From the hill is an excellent view of Llanthony Priory nestling in the Vale of Ewyas.

On reaching the crest of the hillside follow a narrow track on the right, in the direction of the Sugar Loaf mountain, which joins up with a wide path leading down to the twin humps of Graig. Follow the track between two stone walls. Turn right and descend to rejoin your outward route leading back to the church.

Cwmyoy Church (C. Barber)

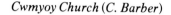

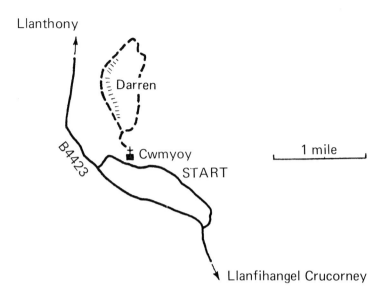

Llanthony

Darren

B4423

Cwmyoy
START

1 mile

Llanfihangel Crucorney

ROUTE 29

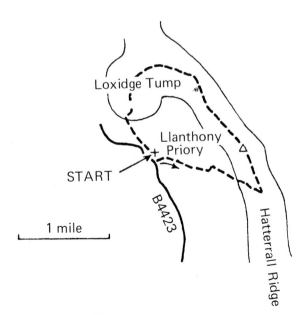

Loxidge Tump

Llanthony
Priory

START

B4423

Hatterrall Ridge

1 mile

ROUTE 30

61

Route 30
Rhiw Cwrw (3 hours)

This route starts from Llanthony Priory and the first part follows an ancient track said to have been made by the priory monks for the purpose of transporting beer across the Hatterrall mountain ridge from the ale house at Longtown in the Craswall Valley.

Nowadays one can enjoy a cool drink in the cellar bar at the Abbey Hotel, and also explore the twelfth century ruins before starting your walk.

From the front of Court Farm follow a track over a stile and around to the rear of the house. Go through a metal gate, bear right and follow a route to the mountain fence via the Wirral Wood. Climb the stile at the fence and bear right. The next section is often boggy but soon the track starts to ascend towards the ridge at a gentle angle. Ahead, to the right, is a fine view of the Sugar Loaf. On the left the walker will pass a wooden wayside cross erected at this spot where the ashes of Mr and Mrs Carslake were scattered. They were regular visitors to the Abbey Hotel.

Continue, with good views behind of Llanthony Priory, to arrive on top of the ridge overlooking the Longtown Valley. From here you may complete the monks' journey by descending the track to Longtown, return by the same route, or continue along the ridge to the north. Soon at an altitude of 1,810ft. a trig' point is reached. In the distance, on the right, is the Cat's Back—a narrow ridge leading up to Black Hill. To the west is a fine view of Pen y Gader Fawr.

After about another mile leave the ridge by a pile of stones and cut across in a westerly direction to follow the contour around the head of Cwm Siarpal. Near the southern end of Loxidge Tump is a broad track leading down in a series of zig-zags to a hill gate near Loxidge cottage. From there follow the waymarked route to Llanthony Priory.

The tiny hamlet of Llanthony is situated in the heart of the Vale of Ewyas, and is famous for its ruined Priory built in the twelfth century on the site of a primitive mud and wattle shrine erected in the sixth century by St. David. The west tower and prior's house are now an hotel, and very cool refreshment may be obtained from the cellar bar situated below ground level.

Route 31
Bâl Mawr and Chwarel y Fan (4 hours)

Leave your car in the Priory car park. From Llanthony village follow a lane to reach a metal footbridge spanning the Afon Honddu. Cross a stile and keep to the right side of the field, another stile, then over a gate opposite. Follow a stream and later cross it to reach Cwm-bwchel Farm. Through a gate in the farmyard and follow waymarks to the open hill. A well worn track leads up the Cwm, providing good views of Llanthony Priory with a

Chwarel y Fan (C. Barber)

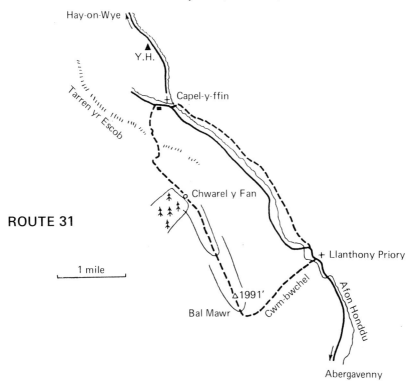

Hay-on-Wye

Y.H.

Capel-y-ffin

Tarren yr Escob

Chwarel y Fan

ROUTE 31

Llanthony Priory

1 mile

△1991'

Bal Mawr

Cwm-bwchel

Afon Honddu

Abergavenny

gradual ascent to the ridge above.

Turn right and follow the track up Bâl Mawr (1,990ft.) to the trig' point and a good view. The ridge leading over Bwlch-bâch is narrow and heather clad. A large cairn is reached at the top of Chwarel y Fan (2,228ft.), and the remains of old quarries provide good shelter from the wind.

Descending from this point another cairn marks the way at "Blacksmiths Anvil". Follow the track to the right, which is cairn marked at intervals, down to the top of Tarren yr Esgob cliffs where a rocky path marked by a cairn perched near the edge of the escarpment provides an easy descent. From the bottom of the steep slope head diagonally to the left to cross a stream and then straight down to a gate at the rear of the Grange Pony Trekking Centre.

The monastery here was founded in 1870 by Father Ignatius. The church lies in ruins but the monastery is now a private house, part of which is open to the public.

Proceed down the drive to turn right and then left at the next road junction to reach Capel-y-ffin village. Beside the churchyard, pass through a metal gate to follow a footpath past the Baptist Chapel and Blaenau House. Follow waymarks to reach a surfaced road. On reaching Tafalog Bridge (276294) leave the road and pass through a wooden gate to follow a path which becomes a surfaced road again near Broadley Farm. Continue to starting point at Llanthony.

Route 32
Tarren yr Esgob, Rhos Dirion, Twmpa and Darren Lŵyd (4½ hours)

Just south of Capel-y-ffin village turn up the road leading to the Nant y Bwch valley. After ¼ mile turn left up the drive leading to the Monastery and turn right to pass the Grange Trekking Centre. Now follow a pony path leading to the hillside above.

A cairn can be seen on the top of the escarpment of Tarren yr Esgob. Follow a rocky track up to this point. From the cairn, head straight up to the crest of the ridge and take its central path to the north-west, looking down on the Grwyne Fawr Reservoir nestling in the valley below. The summit of Twyn Tal-y-cefn (2,303ft.) is marked by a cairn. Continue to the edge of the north escarpment and the trig' point of Rhos Dirion (2,338ft.). From here is an impressive view to the north. Now head north-east and descend to the head of the Nant y Bwch Valley. (A return to Capel-y-ffin can be made by following the track down the valley.) Now a short ascent leads to the summit of Twmpa (2,263ft.) marked by a cairn.

From there follow a track down the ridge to the south-east to shortly pass a cairn marking the top of Darren Lŵyd. This is a very fine viewpoint of the

Capel-y-ffin Monastery from Darren Lŵyd (C. Barber)

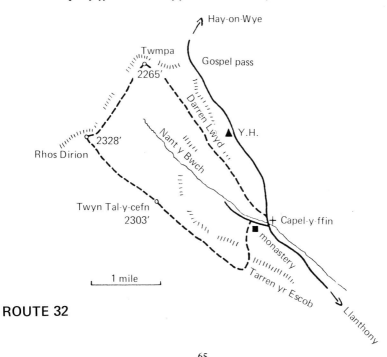

ROUTE 32

beautiful Llanthony Valley. Soon you are above the King George VI Memorial Youth Hostel and a track near the end of the ridge provides a descent route. Two large cairns are reached at the end of the ridge; the second one is perched on the edge and a very steep descent follows between a jumble of rocks. A gate is reached leading to Pen-y-maes farm. Follow a footpath down through a field to reach a stile—turn right and go down the road to the village.

A Walk near Llanveynoe

Route 33
Crib y Garth, "The Cat's Back"
(Short route 2½ hours, long route 4½ hours)

This is a walk up the short narrow easterly ridge of the Black Mountains known locally as the "Cat's Back". It is very similar in character to the Skirrid Fawr ridge and the suggested route may be combined with a section of the Offa's Dyke path on the Hatterrall ridge to give a circuit walk.

Start at the car park/picnic site (288328) near the foot of the Cat's Back just to the north-west of little Black Hill. The way is signposted from the car park to "Black Hill and Offa's Dyke Path". Cross the stile and head up the slope weaving between gorse bushes and hawthorn trees. Soon the ridge above is reached and the gradient is easier. To your left is the Hatterrall ridge carrying Offa's Dyke footpath, and to the right is the more open patchwork-quilt view of Herefordshire. Below is Longtown Valley with Graig Syfyrddin in the distance.

The ridge becomes a series of rocky steps and a cairn is reached near some old quarries which provide good shelter for a lunch stop. From here the ridge narrows for a few hundred yards and then broadens into Black Hill—the summit being marked by a trig' point at 2,101 feet.

Follow a well worn path north-west towards Hay Bluff. Where the track crosses the head of the Olchon Valley the walk may be shortened by following a track down the valley, and then by road back to the start (2½ hours).

The main track continues along the eastern side of the escarpment curving around to join up with the Offa's Dyke path. From here it is a short distance to Hay Bluff, 2,220 feet—marked by a trig' point—where there is a fine view to the north.

Return now along the Offa's Dyke path. A short ascent leads to the high point of 2,306 feet and then a long plod, following a well worn path, brings you to a boundary stone set upright in the middle of the track. Continue for ¼ mile to reach a cairn at 270319. Follow a narrow track to the left and descend the eastern escarpment on an ancient path which zig-zags down the

Northern Escarpment (C. Barber)

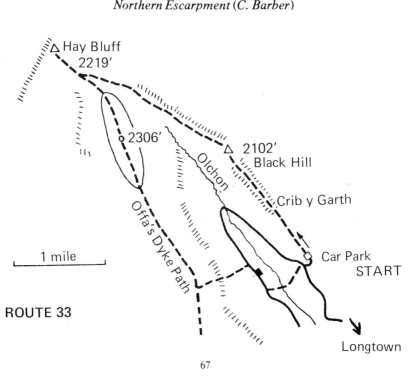

steep slope. On reaching a gate and the road, turn right. Passing Olchon Court you will notice an unusual sign fashioned from horseshoes. A track on the left is soon reached which goes past Beili-bâch Farm, then through a gate and directly down to a footbridge at the junction of two streams. Follow the path to Black Hill Farm and then up a gravel track to a road; turn left and then right to return to the starting point.

Walks near Crickhowell

Route 34
Circuit of the Penn Allt-mawr and Gader ridges
(Strenuous walk—allow 7 hours)

Start at Llanbedr village (240204). Park near the church and follow a lane due east passing old cottages. The tarmac surface soon becomes a rough track descending steeply down to the river Grwyne. Cross a small footbridge and on the other side ascend a steep slope, keeping to the left, to reach a large flat stone that was once a stile. Cross here and continue upwards to reach a road. The village of Llanbedr is now directly below. Turn left and follow the road for nearly a mile. On reaching a gate on the right follow the track up to Draen Farm. Go round the rear of the old building and through a metal gate. Keep straight on by the side of a stone wall and through another metal gate to follow a wide track. At this point there are open views of the Grwyne Fechan Valley. In the distance is Pen y Gader Fawr and behind, to the right, is the Table Mountain (Crug Hywel)—the final point on this walk.

The track now ascends very gradually across the lower slopes of Blaen-yr-henbant with good views of Ysgyryd Fawr and Mynydd Pen-y-fal (the Sugar Loaf). Pass below the summit of Crug Mawr (slight detour to include this point). Soon the open plateau of the ridge is reached, and one can look down on the Grwyne Fawr Valley. At Disgwylfa there is a small cairn.

Keep along the crest of the ridge via Pen Gwllt-meirch (ignore forestry track below) and Pen-tŵyn-mawr (2,153ft.). From here the track continues in a straight line, like a well worn trench to reach the final hump of Pen y Gader Fawr (2,624ft.). This is surely the finest peak of the Black Mountains and is surprisingly lower than the plateau of Waun Fach. A small cairn marks the summit and there is a small stone windbreak.

The track now descends north-west from the summit hump to cross a peaty plateau (often quite boggy) and one has to jump a deep trench near the upper approaches to Waun Fach. People have been known to fall into the trench in the mist.

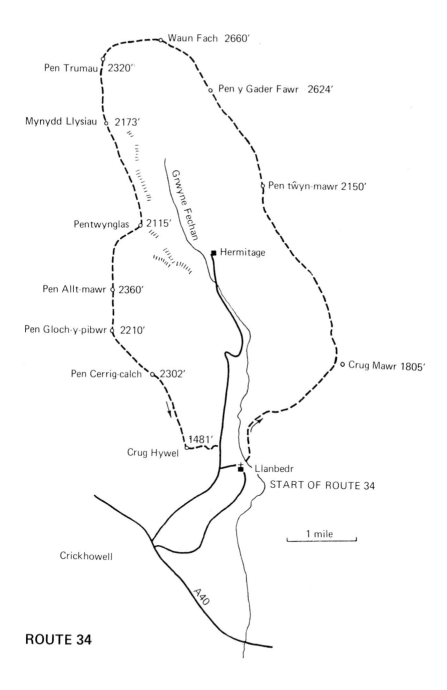

Waun Fach 2660'

Pen Trumau 2320''

Pen y Gader Fawr 2624'

Mynydd Llysiau 2173'

Grwyne Fechan

Pen tŵyn-mawr 2150'

Pentwynglas 2115'

Hermitage

Pen Allt-mawr 2360'

Pen Gloch-y-pibwr 2210'

Crug Mawr 1805'

Pen Cerrig-calch 2302'

1481'

Crug Hywel

Llanbedr

START OF ROUTE 34

1 mile

Crickhowell

A40

ROUTE 34

Grwyne Fechan from Pentwynglas (C. Barber)

Waun Fach summit (2,660ft.) can be difficult to locate in the mist. It is marked by a trig' point base painted white and two cairns. Head west and descend Pen Trumau to reach a large cairn, then a short steep ascent to Mynydd Llysiau (2,173ft.) and follow the edge of the ridge to reach Pentwyn Glas (2,116ft.) with its small summit marked by 19th century boundary stones.

The top of Pen Allt-mawr now looms up in the distance. A large cairn is reached, and from here is the steepest climb on the walk. Ascend directly or follow a diagonal track on the right to the trig' point on the summit at 2,360 feet and a large stone windbreak. Here is a very good viewpoint. Continue passing Gloch-y-pibwr (or make a detour to include its twin cairns) to reach the final peak on the ridge, Pen Cerrig-calch (2,300ft.). The path ascends to this peak past curiously eroded limestone rocks, providing geologists with an interesting problem, for this is the only piece of limestone in the Black Mountains, and was, perhaps, once part of the Llangattock escarpment.

From the trig' point continue in a south-easterly direction to follow a track leading down to the Table Mountain (Crug Hywel) 1,481 feet. Llanbedr is now seen directly below.

Follow a track to the east down to a small building; then through a gate and pass between two buildings to reach another gate. Keep straight on and follow the edge of the field to its bottom left hand corner. On reaching the final gate and the road turn right past Ty Mawr Farm and take the next road on the left which leads to Llanbedr and your starting point.

Route 35
Crug Hywel 1,481 feet (2½ hours)

Crickhowell is dominated by this flat topped Iron Age hill fort, which is popularly known as the Table Mountain. At one time the ancient camp was said to have been the frontier fortress of Hywel Dda (Howell the Good) who was once a well respected Prince of South Wales.

Start at the White Hart Inn (on the north-west side of Crickhowell), by the side of the A40. On the right of the inn a lane ascends steeply. Turn right at the first junction and shortly reach a F.P. sign on the left, then over a stile and along the left side of a field with the Cwmbeth brook gurgling in the dingle below. There is a ruined cottage romantically situated in the dingle. Continue by the side of a wire fence to reach a stile hidden behind a hawthorn tree; through a gate and over another stile—proceed through the dingle and then a metal gate. After crossing a stream follow its left bank—then up the bed of the stream between two stone walls. Pass through two gates and head for the right hand corner of the sheep pen. Follow the stone wall on the right to find a well worn path leading to another stone wall. Keep to the left hand side and soon you will reach the northern end of the Table Mountain, and a scramble up the rocks will take you to the summit. From here there are very fine views of the surrounding mountains.

Descend at the southerly end and head towards the right hand corner of the field below, where the track passes through a metal gate and past Dol-y-gaer house. Now through another gate to immediately cross a stile on the left. Follow waymarks (via further gates and stiles) to reach the Wern Farm; from here a lane leads to a road junction. Turn right and immediately on your right is a green lane which will take you back to the starting point.

Route 36
Craig y Cilau (3½ hours)

Start from Crickhowell bridge, then go through a kissing gate opposite the bridge and follow the path to Llangattock church. This church of St. Catwg's contains stocks and a whipping post. Turn left into the village and then right (ignoring the turning to Beaufort) to follow the road up to the canal. After crossing the canal bridge a clearing is reached a short distance along the road. A car may be left here if one wishes to avoid the initial road walk.

From the clearing (205169) take a track through a gate and walk pleasantly through a wood. High above looms Llangattock escarpment. In certain conditions a double echo may be obtained by shouting at the cliffs above. A steep incline is reached which was once the scene of industrious activity when the quarries were in operation. As you ascend look for the occasional stone with a neat hole in it that was once a tram road sleeper.

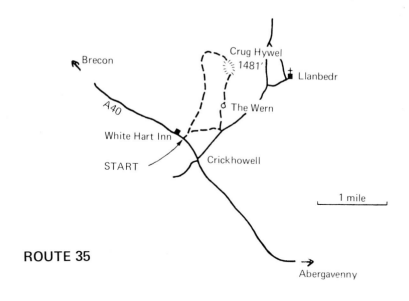

ROUTE 35

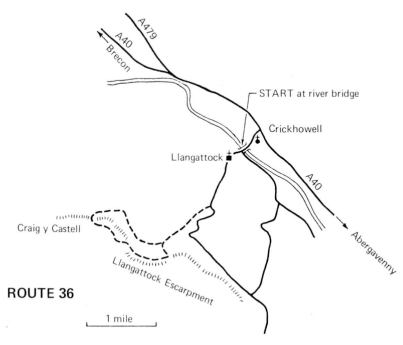

ROUTE 36

On reaching the top of the incline pause to enjoy the view of Crickhowell, Table Mountain and the Pen Allt-mawr ridge of the Black Mountains. By the remains of an old lime kiln the track continues upwards to the left. At the top turn right to follow a level stony track running along the contour of the escarpment. The full panoramic view may now be enjoyed at leisure. Soon the track narrows and the slope below becomes steeper. Far below the rushing waters of the Onneu-fach are heard.

The track broadens as the Craig y Cilau Nature Reserve is entered. Look out for the sign mounted on a rock to the left of the track. This Nature Reserve was established in 1959 and is 157 acres in size, situated at an altitude of between 900 and 1,500 feet. It is noted as the site of some rare trees that include large and small leaved limes and four indigenous species of Sorbus. Two of these are not known outside Powys. One of them is the lesser Whitebeam (Sorbus miniba) which is closely related to the Mountain Ash or Rowan. Several cave systems are also to be found in the Reserve.

As one enters this amphitheatre of cliffs, screes and trees, their beauty and situation cannot fail to impress.

On reaching a little bay the cave system of Eglwys Faen (stone church) can be seen. There are four entrances, but only two are generally used; the first one is to the left of the track. This entrance, a round hole in the cliff face, is reached by a short scramble up the rocky incline which is well polished and can be very slippery in wet weather—so it is expedient to be careful. Around the corner another track leads upwards to the main entrance which gives good access to a big chamber. This is the most suitable entrance for a brief visit.

Continue along the escarpment track. On reaching a stony hollow at the end of the lower escarpment look for a metal door set in the face of the cliff near the base. This is the entrance to Agen Allwed cave system which extends for a total distance of eighteen miles inside the mountain. At one time it was rated the longest cave system in the country. Thirty yards on is the original entrance which is gated further inside; shaped like a keyhole— the translation of Agen Allwed.

The narrow track now continues upwards across a scree slope with an impressive drop below; it ascends gradually, contouring the steep slopes, providing a very fine view of the Usk Valley. It traverses some "airy corners" below the summit ridge until level ground is reached and then goes down to the end of the cliffs where it is possible to descend.

Now follow the track along the base of the cliffs and descend towards Crickhowell until a flat clearing is reached. Continue right, alongside a wire fence, to enter the vale of Cwm Onneu-fach. Keep on the right hand side of the valley bottom and later follow a wire fence and stone wall past the remains of an old lime kiln. Where the stone wall turns into a bay go through a gate, cross a stream and turn right.

Reaching a junction, after a stile, take a track following a wire fence by a stream. Soon cross a stile in the fence and over a stream to join a track on the other side. Follow the right hand side of the stream through Onneu Fach dingle to reach the foot of the incline previously ascended; then return along track to the start of the walk.

Outlying Hills

To the west of the Black Mountains a ridge starts at Bwlch and finishes at Pengenfford. This route features two interesting peaks—Mynydd Llangorse and Mynydd Troed. A road through Cwm Sorgwm passes between them to offer easy access to both hills.

South-west of the Black Mountains, and on the other side of the Usk Valley are the large moorland areas of Mynydd Llangynidr and Mynydd Llangattock. These moors are wide and featureless and should be treated with respect, particularly in bad weather.

There are three hills grouped around Abergavenny, often referred to as The Three Peaks. A popular endurance walk is organised by the Youth Hostels Association every year which traverses these hills and is eighteen miles in distance. The hills are locally known as Sugar Loaf, Blorenge and Skirrid Fawr.

A small hill to the east of Abergavenny is called Ysgyryd Fach (Little Skirrid), an easy walk affording fine viewpoints. Another minor hill to the north of Abergavenny is called Bryn Arw.

The shapely peak to the north of Abergavenny is said to resemble a heap of sugar when poured out of a bag, and so it does when seen from certain points of the compass. It is called Mynydd Pen-y-fal, or to give it its local name, and also one well known to the tourist—the Sugar Loaf. At 1,955 feet it just fails to reach the magic height of 2,000 feet, yet it always seems to be a much higher mountain for the approaches are quite long and the view from the summit is very extensive. There are many interesting ways to the top, and it may be ascended directly from Abergavenny. Lord Hunt, of Everest fame, once visited the area and insisted on climbing it from the north side, although the usual approach is from its southern slopes.

The summit is about three hundred yards long and there is a cluster of rocks at the western end. The extensive view ranges from the large mass of the Black Mountains to the north, the Usk Valley beyond Crickhowell with the Brecon Beacons in the far distance; Ysgyryd Fawr and the rich farmland stretching east to the Malverns and the Cotswold Hills. The whole of Abergavenny with the river Usk winding its way towards the Severn Estuary can be seen. To the south is the bulky mass of the Blorenge, and on its right the limestone gorge of Clydach containing the Heads of the Valleys road. Three popular routes to the summit are as follows.

The Sugar Loaf from the north-west (C. Barber)

Route 37
Mynydd Pen-y-fal from Mynydd Llanwenarth car park (2 hours)

This is the shortest route up the Sugar Loaf and starts from the viewpoint car park at G.R.268167. The car park is reached by turning right into Pentre Lane from the A40 half a mile west of Abergavenny. Follow signs to the summit of the Sugar Loaf.

From the car park a well defined track leads along the curved ridge of Mynydd Llanwenarth to reach the summit of the Sugar Loaf by the south-west slope.

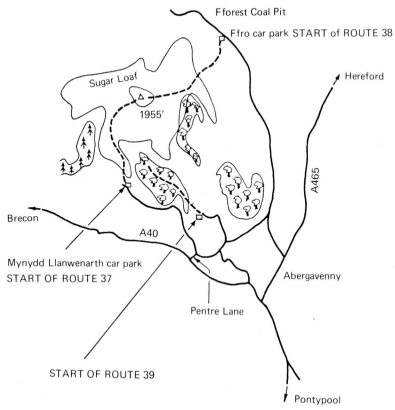

ROUTES 37, 38 and 39

Route 38
Mynydd Pen-y-fal from Ffro car park
(2½ hours)

To reach this car park at G.R.291201 take the old Hereford road from Abergavenny to Pant-y-Gelli. Turn left for Bettws and the car park is on the left hand side, approximately one mile beyond Bettws church. A well defined track ascends the north-eastern slopes, or one may join the main track at Twyn Gwyn and thence to the summit.

Route 39
St. Mary's Vale Nature Trail (1½ hours)

Approximately one and a half miles from Abergavenny is St. Mary's Vale which is the setting for a nature trail established by the Brecon Beacons National Park Authority, on National Trust property.

The trail starts at G.R.284162. This point is reached by leaving the Brecon Road in Abergavenny and following Chapel Road to join Pentre Road. Travel northwards to pass Llwyn-du Reservoir on the right to take the next turning left which leads to the start of the trail. Parking is limited.

The route of the trail and observations at seven stopping places are described in detail in an Information Sheet which is available from any Brecon Beacons National Park Information Centre.

Route 40
Ysgyryd Fawr—1,595 feet—The Holy Mountain (2½ hours)

Start at the small car park on B4521 approximately three miles north-east of Abergavenny (G.R.329164). Walk thirty yards from the car park towards Abergavenny to cross a stile signposted "Skirrid Fawr", and continue straight up the side of the field. In a corner of the adjoining field cross a stile to the path going upwards through the Skirrid wood to a series of steps. At the end of the Forestry plantation cross a stile and then turn right to pass through a picturesque dingle to reach a junction and a waymarked route to the open hill.

On joining the ridge the view opens up on both sides. The ridge is approximately one mile in length with an easy gradient all the way. The trig' point is seen at the far end. On the west side are steep cliffs where a massive landslip left a deep cutting. Local legend says alternatively that this was caused by Noah's ark grounding on the mountain; it was a giant's footprint; or that it was due to an earthquake at the time of the crucifixion of Christ, when the "rocks were rent". On the summit are traces of St. Michael's Chapel and two upright stones were possibly part of the entrance. The panoramic views from the summit are very impressive.

If the walker is not happy about steep descents he should return by his outward route, otherwise descend the steep northern slope. At the foot of the slope follow a track leading into the landslide valley. Notice a strange toadstool-shaped rock—The Devil's Table—on the hillside above. The path leads pleasantly down through the valley and then ascends slightly through the woods at the southern end of the hill. Rejoin the original path and return to the starting point.

Ysgyryd Fawr from the north-east (C. Barber)

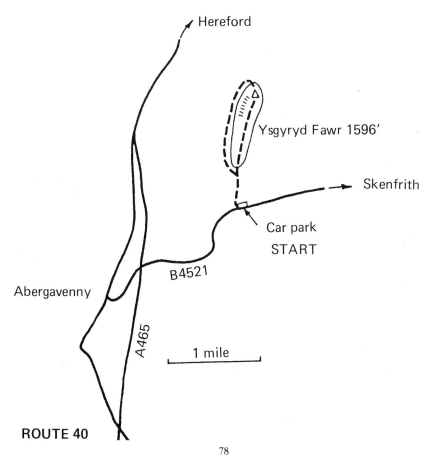

Hereford

Ysgyryd Fawr 1596'

Skenfrith

Car park

START

B4521

Abergavenny

A465

1 mile

ROUTE 40

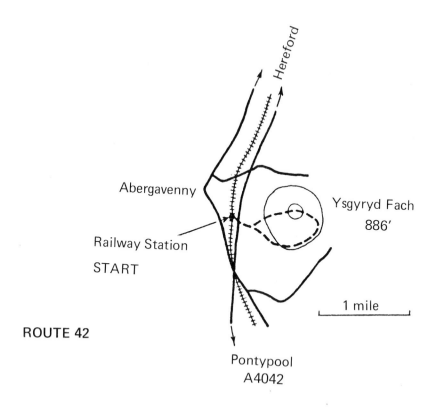

Hereford

Abergavenny

Ysgyryd Fach
886'

Railway Station

START

1 mile

ROUTE 42

Pontypool
A4042

Route 41
Ascent of the Blorenge (3½ hours)

Start from Llanfoist village to the south-west of Abergavenny. Follow the Llanellen road (B4269) and turn off to the right up a lane that climbs steeply up the hillside to cross a canal bridge. The road continues upwards past three farms. At the third farm, Upper Ninfa, turn right up a steep track which later joins the Blaenavon mountain road. Near a cattle grid follow the road west for a quarter of a mile to reach a track on the right. Go north for half a mile to reach the Blorenge summit at 1,833 feet. Having enjoyed the view of the Usk Valley and the Black Mountains head north-east to reach the steep end of the Blorenge. Now descend the north east shoulder where a steep track from the disused firing range leads down through a wooded valley to pass through a fascinating tunnel under the canal near the old wharf at Llanfoist.

In the bed of the canal cannon balls and shot of various sizes were once found. Such loads were lowered on trams down the incline to the waiting barges for use in the Napoloenic wars. A bronze Age axe was also found here by two schoolboys.

Route 42
Ysgyryd Fach - Little Skirrid (1½ hours)

Ysgyryd Fach is a conical shaped hill to the south-east of Abergavenny. It is nine hundred feet in height and wooded on all sides.

Park at Abergavenny railway station and cross a footbridge over the lines to follow a waymarked path for one hundred yards towards a signal box. Cross the main Hereford road to ascend some concrete steps and a stile on the other side. The path now follows the edge of a deep stream gully. At the top of the gully cross a bridge, climb a stile and cross a field to reach a stile in its top left hand corner. Soon after cross another stile and take the track up through the trees. On reaching a junction keep straight on up a series of steps through a leafy dingle past two track junctions. Continue straight on following the side of a fence to finally reach the top of the hill where a seat is provided. The view is particularly rewarding as it provides a wide panoramic view of the Usk Valley, the Blorenge, Sugar Loaf, Ysgyryd Fawr and the Black Mountains.

Having enjoyed the view walk to the south of the summit and follow a track through the trees for about half a mile; there the wood ends and the track broadens to skirt the edge of the wood in a westerly direction until it reaches the "Keeper's Cottage". Turn right and cross a stone footbridge and then a stile. Keep the hedge on your left to reach another stile. Over this to follow the track alongside a stream to the next stile. At this point you join the outward route to the starting point.

Route 43
Bryn Arw (2 hours)

Bryn Arw is an isolated hill to the east of the Sugar Loaf. It is not very high and its ascent does not present much of a challenge, but it is worth the climb for the fine viewpoint it offers.

Start from the Fro car park G.R.291201 on the north-eastern side of the Sugar Loaf near Fforest Coal Pit. Walk down the road, south-east, and take the first left turning which leads to Rhyd Farm. Above the farm follow a track to reach the ridge above. From here pleasant views may be enjoyed. Follow the ridge in a northerly direction and then descend on the north-west side to join a track just above a stone wall. This path shortly meets a wide track above Cwm Coedycerrig. Take a left turn here and soon a tarmac road is reached; after fifty yards further turn left through a metal gate—sign-

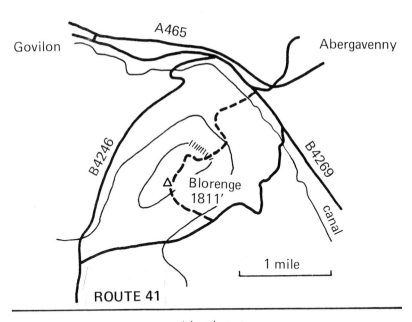

Govilon A465 Abergavenny

B4246 B4269

Blorenge
1811'

canal

1 mile

ROUTE 41

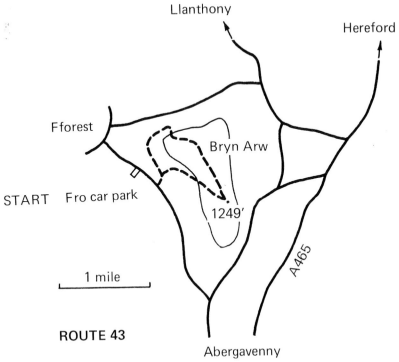

Llanthony

Hereford

Fforest

Bryn Arw

START Fro car park

1249'

A465

1 mile

ROUTE 43

Abergavenny

posted Bettws. Follow this path for about three-quarters of a mile to reach the road, then turn right to arrive back at the car park starting point.

Route 44
Mynydd Llangynidr—The Chartists' Cave (3 hours)

Leave your car at a car park, situated G.R.156172. Walk up the Beaufort road to reach a gravel track on the right. This leads to a small abandoned quarry with a smooth rock floor; a cave entrance resembling the mouth of a railway tunnel can be seen in the rock face of the quarry. This is Blaen Onneu cave which extends for about one hundred and fifty feet and should be examined with care. On the right hand side of the quarry floor is a pot-hole covered by a boulder—to prevent sheep or careless walkers dropping inside.

Scramble up a sheep track to the left of the cave to the open moor above. Now walk in a south-westerly direction until a prominent cairn is sighted. On reaching this trig' point, G.R.148159, at a spot height of 1,773 feet, should be visible. In poor visibility a compass bearing from the quarry to the

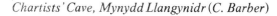

Chartists' Cave, Mynydd Llangynidr (C. Barber)

82

ROUTE 44

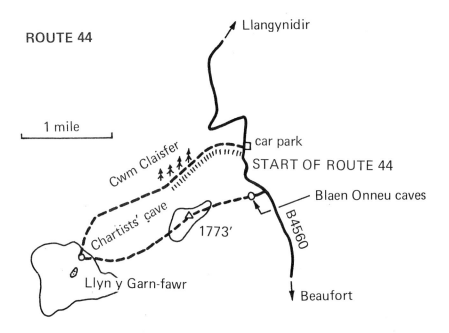

Llangynidir

1 mile

Cwm Claisfer

car park

START OF ROUTE 44

Blaen Onneu caves

Chartists' cave

1773'

B4560

Llyn y Garn-fawr

Beaufort

trig' point should be taken. From there follow a path towards Garn Fawr which appears as a hump on the ridge two miles away. (In poor visibility walk on a compass bearing directly to The Chartists' Cave.) The path soon disappears and numerous swallet holes are passed on this route. These circular depressions are caused by the roofs of underground chambers collapsing.

On reaching Garn Fawr, 1,805 feet, walk north-east to reach a low cliff where The Chartists' Cave may be found. The entrance is about six feet high below a rock arch, G.R.127153. Inside is a chamber providing excellent shelter and two passages leading to other smaller chambers. The cave was reputed to have been used by the Chartists in the 19th century as a meeting place and ammunition store prior to their historic march on Newport in 1838. It is mentioned in the novel "Rape of the Fair Country" by Alexander Cordell.

One may either return by the same route or by the following alternative to give variety to the walk.

Head in a north-easterly direction to reach the rim of Blaen Cwm-claisfer. Contour around the heather-covered and rocky slopes to reach the base of a limestone escarpment, then follow a track alongside a stone wall above the forestry plantation to reach an old tram road leading past the

Blaen Onneu quarries. On reaching a tarmac road turn left and return to the starting point.

N.B.: It should be emphasised that care should be taken in this area during misty weather and without the help of a compass (and the ability to use it) for it is possible for walkers to lose sense of direction and exhaust themselves walking in circles.

Route 45
Mynydd Llangorse and Mynydd Troed
(Allow 40 minutes for each peak)

These two peaks are situated to the west of the Black Mountains, and a few miles south of Talgarth. They are both easily climbed from a convenient parking spot at the summit of the road leading up Cwm Sorgwm from the Crickhowell - Talgarth road, A479.

Near a convenient parking area G.R. 161284 at the top of Cwm Sorgwm are three small stones. These are not gravestones as so many people believe, but are stones marking the boundaries of three 19th century land-owners. From here well worn tracks lead directly to the summits of Mynydd Troed (1,997ft.) and Mynydd Llangorse (1,661ft.), which are excellent viewpoints.

For a longer walk to the two summits start from the village of Bwlch (G.R.149220) on the A40 and follow a well defined path over Cefn Moel to reach Mynydd Llangorse and Mynydd Troed.

★ ★ ★ ★

ROUTE 45

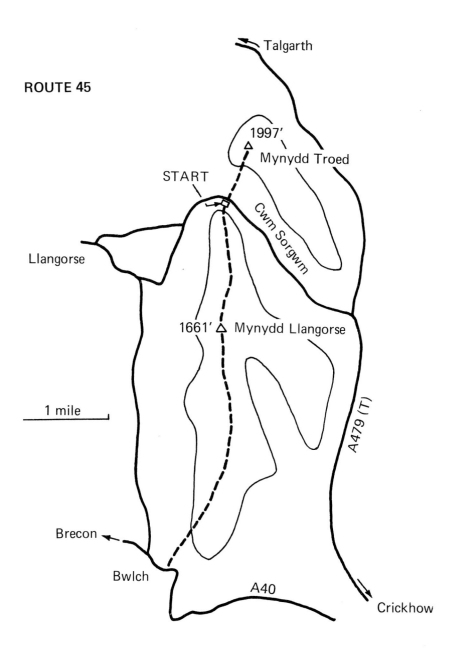

Youth Hostels

There are five Youth Hostels in the Brecon Beacons National Park. They are Ty'n-y-caeau, Llwyn-y-celyn, Llanddeusant, Ystradfellte and Capel-y-ffin.

Ty'n-y-caeau, 2½ miles east of Brecon, has accommodation for 61 people. Address: Ty'n-y-caeau, Groesfford, Brecon, Powys. Tel. (087486) 270.

Llwyn-y-celyn, 6 miles from Brecon on the Merthyr road, is an old farm house recently restored by volunteers. It is in a beautiful and peaceful situation. It has accommodation for 50 people. Address: Llwyn-y-celyn, Libanus, Brecon, Powys. Tel. (0874) 4261.

Llanddeusant, 7 miles south of Llandovery, is best approached from the Trecastle - Llangadog mountain road. The Carmarthen Fans are in easy reach from the Hostel. It has accommodation for 36 people. Address: The Old Red Lion. Llanddeusant, Llangadog, Dyfed. Tel. (05504) 677.

Ystradfellte, 5 miles north of Pont Nedd Fechan. This Hostel is well situated for walkers wishing to explore the magnificent waterfalls and caves in this area. It is a simple Hostel, with accommodation for 26 people. Address: Tai'r Heol, Ystradfellte, Aberdare, Mid Glamorgan. Tel. (0639) 720301.

Capel-y-ffin Youth Hostel (C. Barber)

Capel-y-ffin, 8 miles south of Hay on Wye. Situated at an altitude of 1,300 feet the building is an old farmhouse converted into a comfortable Hostel with money made available to the Y.H.A. by the King George VI Memorial Trust. It has accommodation for 38 people.
Address: The Youth Hostel, Capel-y-ffin, Abergavenny, Gwent. Tel. (087382) 373.

South Wales Regional Office. Regional Secretary, 131 Woodville Road, Cardiff, South Glamorgan, CF2 4DZ. Tel. (0222) 31370.

Camping

There are very few official camping sites in this area, but landowners are sometimes willing to allow camping on their land. Much of the open mountain land of the Brecon Beacons is owned by the National Trust which does not generally permit camping. It must be emphasised that you can not camp where you please; permission should always be sought. Details of a few popular camping sites are given below, but up to date information of caravan and camping sites may be obtained from the Brecon Beacons National Park Information Centres, listed on the last page.

BRECON BEACONS

Cwm Llwch — There are several good sites near the parking area at G.R.006246. Obtain permission from Modrydd Farm, near Libanus.

Talybont Reservoir — G.R.105210. Tel. (Reservoir Superintendent) Talybont-on-Usk 237.

BLACK MOUNTAINS

Capel-y-ffin — Chapel Farm.

Crickhowell — Riverside Caravan Park, New Road. Tel. Crickhowell 397.

Llanwenarth Citra — Pysgodlyn Farm, Abergavenny, Gwent. Tel. Abergavenny 3271.

Pandy — The Rising Sun Inn. Tel. Crucorney 254.

Rock Climbing

*Climb if you will, but remember that courage and strength
are nought without prudence. . . .*

Edward Whymper

The rock climber finds little scope in the Brecon Beacons because the loose
and friable Old Red Sandstone is not suitable for the sport. However
tempting the north-east face of Pen y Fan may look its crumbling edges and
gullies are best left alone. Sandeman, an experienced climber from Abergavenny, is believed to have made the first winter ascent of the north-east
face in 1939, and his record of the climb leaves would-be imitators in no
doubt of the difficulties.

The Black Mountains do not offer any scope for the rock climber either.
However tempting the steep Darren cliffs at Cwmyoy, and above Longtown, may look, their insecure and crumbling faces should be left well
alone.

Climbing on carboniferous limestone is much more satisfactory, and
routes of all standards can be found on some of the old quarry faces in the
National Park. The most popular are those at Mynydd Llangattock, near
Crickhowell, Coed-y-cymmer, Morlais, Taf Fechan, Twynau Gwynion,
near Merthyr Tydfil, and Dinas rock near Pont Nêdd Fechan.

For further information consult the rock climbing guide to South East
Wales, published by the South Wales Mountaineering Club.

Right-hand gully, north-east face of Pen y Fan (C. Barber)

Caving

South Wales is now a very popular caving area. Large numbers of speleologists visit the limestone outcrops of the Brecon Beacons National Park to explore the subterranean systems and search for new ones.

Caving is not for the solitary explorer; anyone attracted to it should contact a recognised caving club. Details of local caving clubs can be obtained from The Secretary, South Wales Caving Club, Powell Street,· Penwyllt, Swansea Valley, West Glamorgan.

The following is a brief description of some of the cave systems to be found in the areas covered by this guide.

NEDD VALLEY

Bridge Cave. Length 600 feet. G.R.912140. Entrance is on the left bank just below bridge. The cave is liable to flood. Great care is needed when negotiating boulder ruckle in the entrance passage. Permission should be sought from Blaen-nedd-isaf Farm.

Little Neath River Cave. Length 12,500 feet. G.R.912142. Entrance on left bank about five hundred feet upstream from bridge. Complex system, and entrance liable to flood. Permission as for Bridge Cave.

Pant Mawr Pot. Length 3,700 feet. G.R.891162. Entrance by way of a Yorkshire type pothole nearly eighty feet deep on the mountain to the west of river. The entry is by way of a steep sided swallet hole—a sixty feet caving ladder being required. Below is a slope of boulders leading to a large main passage with good formations. Permission should be sought from South Wales Caving Club.

Cwm Pwll y Rhyd. Length 60 feet. G.R.912137. Situated in Pwll y Rhyd chasm. Large railway tunnel-like entrance from which the Nedd flows. It takes its name from a stalagmite figure which resembles a seated woman.

Town Drain. Length 1,400 feet. G.R.911135. Sometimes known as Arcade Cave. Entrance on eastern side of river bed, just below White Lady cave. Very narrow system of passages with tight squeezes and tortuous bends. Sometimes floods.

MELLTE VALLEY

Porth yr Ogof. Length 2,000 feet. G.R. 927124. Easily entered through large main entrance as described in Route 18.

SYCHRYD VALLEY

Ogof Bwa Maen. Length 210 feet. G.R.913075. Entrance in large opening under Bwa Maen rock. Large chamber and sections of narrow passages leading to two small chambers.

Will's Hole. Length 500 feet. G.R.914080. Entrance in left side of gorge under a ramp leading to the old silica mines. A fifty foot ladder pitch leads to two passages which contain some formations. Specialised knowledge and equipment necessary.

MYNYDD LLANGATTOCK

There are several caves to be found on the Mynydd Llangattock escarpment. The most important is Agen Alwedd which was first explored in 1946, and later extended by the Hereford Caving Club in 1957.

Agen Alwedd. Length approximately 18 miles. G.R.188158. Entrance at the west end of the Llangattock tram road which contours the hillside below the limestone cliffs. There are, in fact, two entrances and both are gated. Permission to enter must be sought from the secretary of the cave management committee, and is only given to members of approved caving clubs. The system of passages inside the cave is very extensive and the exploration of the "Summertime Series" is a serious undertaking.

Eglwys Faen. Length approximately 4,000 feet. G.R.192156. The entrance is about half a mile west of Agen Alwedd and close to the old tram road. The main entrance leads directly into a large chamber from which passages lead in three directions and three different levels of the cave can be explored. There are no formations of any interest, but it is a useful cave for introducing novices to the sport.

Ogof y Darren Cilau. Length approximately 2,500 feet. G.R.206153. Entrance situated about three-quarters of a mile before Eglwys Faen and just above an old lime kiln. It consists mostly of a long wet, and very tight, passage leading to a fairly large main passage with formations. This cave is rated 'severe' and should be treated seriously.

Ogof Pen Eryr. Length approximately 1,200 feet. G.R.208152. Entrance is above the old tram road to the east of the last cave. It consists of a series of tight passages and small chambers. It is very loose in places, and should again be treated with respect and experienced leadership is necessary.

THE CLYDACH GORGE

Ogof Clogwyn. Length 540 feet. G.R.212124. Entrance on the south bank of the river Clydach, about a quarter of a mile above the Devil's Bridge. One has to climb on to an overhanging shelf to enter the cave. Inside is an active stream passage and some fine examples of phreatic shelving throughout its length.

Shakespeare's Cave. Length approximately 1,200 feet. G.R.217126. Entrance is on the north bank of the river Clydach about a quarter of a mile east of the Devil's Bridge. It consists of a single passage which becomes blocked by water after a few hundred feet. Progress beyond this point has been made by those with diving equipment.

Sugar Loaf from Mynydd Llangattock Escarpment (W. T. Barber)

CAVE RESCUE

In the event of a caving accident, notify the police and ask for the local Cave Rescue Organisation to be alerted. Give fullest details and location and circumstances of the accident.

Summits of the Brecon Beacons National Park

	feet	metres
Carmarthen Fans		
Bannau Brecheiniog	2,630	802
Bannau Sir Gaer	2,460	750
Fan Hir	2,366	721
Twyn Swnd	2,011	633
Moel Garnach	2,022	616
Foel Fraith	1,982	604
Fforest Fawr		
Fan Fawr	2,409	734
Fan Gihirych	2,379	725
Fan Nedd	2,176	663
Fan Fraith	2,164	655
Fan Llia	2,071	631
Brecon Beacons		
Pen y Fan	2,907	886
Corn Du	2,863	873
Duwynt	2,704	824
Cribin	2,608	795
Craig Pwllfa	2,504	763
Craig y Fan ddu	2,224	678
Allt-lwyd	2,100	645
Twyn Mwyalchod	2,089	642
Y Gyrn	2,010	613
Fan Big	1,961	598
Pant y Creigiau	1,853	565
Bryn	1,842	561
Outlying Hills of Brecon Beacons		
Tor y Foel	1,806	550
Pen y Crug	1,088	331
Buckland Hill	1,038	316
Black Mountains		
Waun Fach	2,660	810
Pen y Gader Fawr	2,624	800
Pen y Manllwyn	2,500	762
Pen Allt-mawr	2,360	719

	feet	metres
Rhos Dirion	2,338	713
Pen Trumau	2,320	707
Spot height on Hatterrall ridge	2,306	703
Twyn Tal-y-cefn	2,303	702
Pen Cerrig-calch	2,302	701
Twmpa	2,263	690
Y Das	2,232	680
Chwarel y Fan	2,228	679
Hay Bluff	2,219	677
Mynydd Llysiau	2,173	662
Pen Gloch-y-pibwr	2,155	657
Pen-tŵyn-mawr	2,150	655
Pentwynglas	2,115	645
Black Hill	2,102	640
Spot height on Hatterrall ridge	2,091	612
Spot height on Hatterrall ridge	2,000	610

Outlying Hills of Black Mountains

Mynydd Troed	1,997	609
Sugar Loaf	1,955	596
Blorenge	1,833	552
Mynydd Llangynidr	1,805	550
Mynydd Llangattock	1,735	529
Mynydd Llangorse	1,661	508
Ysgyryd Fawr	1,595	486
Bryn Arw	1,200	381
Ysgyryd Fach	850	270

The Three Peaks Trial

The Three Peaks Trial is an eighteen mile endurance walk organised every year by the Youth Hostels Association. First held in 1963, it generally takes place in March and starts from Abergavenny.

The route involves the ascent of the Blorenge, Sugar Loaf and Ysgyryd Fawr mountains. Further information can be obtained from the South Wales Regional Y.H.A. Office, 131 Woodville Road, Cardiff, Glamorgan.

The South Wales Marathon Walk

This is a forty-seven mile endurance walk organised by the Youth Hostels Association, and held in the early summer every year. The walk starts at Llandeusant Youth Hostel near the Carmarthen Fans and finishes at Capel-y-ffin Hostel in the Black Mountains. Sometimes the walk is organised in both directions, and twenty-five walkers start from each end of the route.

The route includes the seven highest peaks of the Brecon Beacons National Park, and the average time taken to complete the walk is about sixteen hours. A description of the walk is given here.

From Llanddeusant Youth Hostel follow the road to the lake of Llyn y Fan fach. In misty weather a compass bearing may be needed to reach the first peak—Bannau Brycheiniog, sometimes referred to as the Carmarthen Fan. From the summit—2,630 feet—descend to Bwlch y Giedd, where a gap in the steep escarpment gives access to a useful track leading to Llyn y Fan fawr. From here head due east to reach the first check point at the Cray Dam.

Leaving Cray the way is then across the wilderness of Fforest Fawr. Make for the ridge of Bwlch y Duwynt and contour around to the next check point at Llethr (on the road at 1,450 feet). Now continue across tufty moorland and boggy ground to pass over the lower slopes of Fan Fawr and down to a check point and feeding station at Storey Arms.

Ascend the Beacons by the 'tourist track' which starts from the roadside nearly a mile to the south of Storey Arms. Scramble up the summit rocks of Corn Du and on to Pen y Fan, 2,907 feet, the highest point of the walk. Continue over Cribin, 2,608 feet, and then across the Roman road to follow the northern escarpment of the Beacons terminating at Craig Pwllfa, 2,504 feet. Descend via Bryn to Llanfrynach and carry on to the check point and feeding station at the Usk bridge, Cefn Brynich.

The next check point is eight miles away at Pengenfford. Care should be taken with the map reading on this section, for a wrong turning will mean extra miles. All entrants are required to arrive at this check point by 7.30 p.m. Failure to do so will mean disqualification for safety reasons.

From Pengenfford ascend the ridge of Y Grîb to reach the featureless plateau of Waun Fach, 2,660 feet, and shortly afterwards Pen y Gader Fawr, 2,624 feet. It is during these last gruelling miles that the challenge of the walk is really felt. and hidden reserves of willpower are eagerly sought. Care should be taken when descending the steep escarpment of Tarren yr Escob overlooking Capel-y-ffin. A large cairn marks the top of the track. On reaching the village a short road walk brings you to the end of the long journey to the comfortable hostel of Capel-y-ffin.

This forty-seven mile walk was first completed on Saturday, 17th May, 1947, in about seventeen hours, by Elwyn Evans, Harry Wills and George Tuffs. In 1958 it was organised as an endurance test for experienced walkers, and arranged by the Youth Hostels Association as an annual event.

Since 1958 countless walkers have taken part in the event; most of them have completed the course successfully—often after two attempts—but there are many who are proud of a 'hat trick'. Three times is enough to convince most marathoners that they *do* have stamina and willpower. However, one enthusiast, Neville Tandy, has to date completed the walk no less than eleven times!

In 1960, John Taylor from London, astonished everybody by completing a double journey involving the incredible distance of ninety-four miles in two days. The first winter crossing was made in 1962 by three members of the Newport Y.H.A. Group, inspired by the leadership of Dave Mathews and supported (not literally) by some thirty helpers and checkers.

In addition, the route has been crossed by 'rough stuff' cyclists in both directions. Following this accomplishment the organisers found it necessary to clamp down on over-energetic entrants by disqualifying double trips, and unusual modes of transport. No doubt most entrants would agree that one receives sufficient personal gratification, and blisters, by simply completing the route on foot—a mere forty-seven miles!

★   ★   ★   ★

Reach for your boots and head for the sky!

Information Centres

Abergavenny, Gwent. Brecon Beacons National Park and South Wales Tourism Coucil Centre, 2 Lower Monk Street. Tel. (0873) 3254.

Brecon, Powys. Brecon Beacons National Park, Watton Mount. Tel. (0874) 4437.

Brecon Beacons Mountain Centre, near Libanus, Brecon. Tel. (0874) 3366.

Llandovery, Dyfed. Brecon Beacons National Park, Central Car Park, 8 Broad Street. Tel. (0550) 20693.

★　★　★　★　★

WEATHER INFORMATION

A local forecast may be obtained from the Brecon Beacons Mountain Centre. Tel. Brecon 3366 after 10.00 am (not in the evening). Or ring the Cardiff Weather Centre. Tel. Cardiff (0222) 397020.

EMERGENCY

Walking or Caving accidents. Phone 999 and ask for Police. They will contact the appropriate rescue service.

Forest or heath fire. Phone 999 and ask for Fire Service.

In both cases, give the Ordnance Survey Grid Reference if possible.